ROBIN'S RHYMES

ROBIN'S RHYMES
By W. G. LYTTLE

The Author.

The Author as "Robin."

And further poetry from the works of Wesley Greenhill Lyttle

in both Ulster-Scots

and

English

ROBIN'S RHYMES
Poems in Ulster-Scots and English

by

WG Lyttle

Edited and compiled by
AG Lyttle

Robin's Rhymes

Published by AG Lyttle

Typographical presentation, Foreword, Introduction, Notes, Glossary © 2021 AG Lyttle

First edition, November 2021
Printed by Kindle Direct Publishing

ISBN: 979-8-7419-4086-0
Imprint: Independently published

Dedicated to the talented poets of Ulster, Scotland and beyond who celebrate the Ulster-Scots language by continuing to write in the Hamely Tongue.

Contents

Contents

ACKNOWLEDGEMENTS

I wish to thank Belfast poet, Gaynor Kane for graciously agreeing to provide the foreword to this new anthology and for her helpful advice—and for spotting some errant typos! My thanks are due, also, to Heather McGuicken, Curator of the North Down Museum and Leanne Briggs for allowing me access to three ledgers of newspaper clippings—many from the old *North Down Herald*—to source some of the text included in this volume. And to Mark Thompson for providing a photograph of his whisky flagon of Heather Dew. Thanks, also, to the unsung heroes of digitalisation, who have made hundreds of newspaper archives readily available online, an invaluable resource to researchers like myself. And finally, my undying thanks to Anita Lyttle, for her skills in proofreading the manuscript. Inevitably, I expect, a few mistakes will have escaped all our diligennce, for which I can only apologise and take full responsibility.

FOREWORD

by Gaynor Kane, poet

"Long live the Ballyboley boys, and flourish evermore;
And long live Wullie Yeaman, the Mayor of Carrowdore,
Who rubs his mare with wisps of notes when he's for Newton boun'
No richer man lives anywhere in all broad County Down."

This extract from a poem recited by Dominie Harvey, the local schoolmaster in WG Lyttle's book, *Sons of the Sod,* has particular significance for me. The late 19th century writer of prose and verse, in both English and Ulster-Scots, was well-known for including real people in his stories and it is pleasing to know that my own great-great-great-grandfather, Wullie Yeaman was a character worthy of inclusion and acquainted with WG Lyttle. So, I feel a personal connection with the poems and am both pleased and honoured to write this foreword.

My interest, as a reader and a poet, is deepened by having lived in Kircubbin, in the Ards Peninsula, for sixteen years before moving back to Belfast. I have experienced the ready welcome of the villagers who soon became great friends. It was a close, friendly community—exactly as we see portrayed in WG Lyttle's writings about the people from that same area a century before and therefore the poems have great resonance.

This book is noteworthy for a number of reasons. By searching for poems within different publications and bringing them together AG Lyttle has created an important anthology. Much of the poetic works of WG Lyttle have been out of print for a hundred years; now they may be enjoyed by new generations of readers. AG (himself, a direct descendent of WG) has added editorial comment as introductions to each poem. Some lend understanding as to what may have inspired WG to write them, others offer cultural and historical context. By having these poems collated, they add value to each other, each one adding some more paint to the local landscape. They form an overarching narrative and allow readers to immerse themselves in WG Lyttle's world and, in particular, that of his alter-ego, Robin Gordon, to see it through his eyes and hear it in his tongue.

Lyttle writes well-crafted poems with structured rhyme schemes and consistent rhythms. Many of the poems are about specific people or places, whilst often being a social or political commentary, also. As WG puts it, himself, in the poem, 'The Old Town Clock':

> *Life is made up of glimpses of pleasures and pain…*

These glimpses show us life, its ups and downs, in Ards, Bangor and surrounding areas at the time. More so, I feel these poems embrace the people they were written for. They are not highbrow or academic. They are poems for the working class. Poems full of energy, romance, satire and comedy, poems which celebrate town and country and honour the locals and the language they spoke.

Which brings me to another reason why this anthology is significant. Several of the poems are written in the vernacular, the Hamely Tongue, capturing the language, as it was spoken by the people who spoke it. As such, it will be a great resource for anyone interested in linguistics and the history of Ulster-Scots. It's worth noting that the book is dedicated to those 'continuing to write in the Hamely Tongue.' Indeed, this book comes at a time when Ulster-Scots is enjoying a renaissance with many contemporary writers choosing to continue the literary traditions laid down by the late eighteenth century bards and rhyming weavers and the nineteenth century 'kailyard' novelists.

AG Lyttle is to be congratulated for bringing these poems together in print for the first time and I hope that many readers will enjoy WG Lyttle's poetry as much as I have.

Gaynor Kane
Belfast
2021

[Gaynor Kane is indeed a direct descendant, through her grandmother, Catherine Yeaman, of Wullie Yeaman of Carrowdore, a local character known to Lyttle and mentioned a number of times in his book, *Sons of the Sod*. Gaynor is a poet from East Belfast whose full collection, *Venus in Pink Marble* was published in 2020 by The Hedgehog Poetry Press, who have previously published three pamphlets/chapbooks of her verse. (See her at www.gaynorkane.com; Twitter @gaynorkane; Facebook @gaynorkanepoet; Instagram @gaynorkanepoet)–Ed.]

INTRODUCTION

Wesley Greenhill Lyttle was a celebrated, late-19th century, Ulster newspaper proprietor, writer, poet and raconteur. He enjoyed much local fame with his widely acclaimed stage appearances reading his own comic short stories, frequently in the broad Ulster-Scots of North Down and Antrim. Nowadays, WG Lyttle—or WG, as he is still often affectionately known—is probably best remembered for his most popular novel, *Betsy Gray*, about the 1798 rebellion in Ireland. But, as well as a writer of prose, he was also an accomplished poet. His poems, whether written in Ulster-Scots or standard English, were often comedic but some were full of pathos or romance.

Now, for the first time, an anthology of his poetry has been compiled, gathering together poems from his various books of short stories and novels and from the newspaper archives. Fittingly, its launch coincides with the publication of WG's long overdue biography, *The Storyteller.*[1]

Some of the poems were written as entertainments that he read at public gatherings—the dignified editor of Bangor's first newspaper showing the lighter side of his character. Others were incorporated within his

---

[1]*The Storyteller,* AG Lyttle, 2021, is available on Amazon.

novels and short stories and many of these are written in the Ulster-Scots of his alter-ego, "Robin Gordon of Ballycuddy."

WG would dress up as "Robin", an elderly country farmer with a full head of grey hair and a bushy beard, to perform his stories on stage. Wherever he appeared, the naïve "Robin" instantly endeared himself to his audiences, whether telling his yarns or reciting his poems.

I trust that this new anthology of my great-grandfather's poetry will prove equally endearing to new and existing fans of his work and to all lovers of the Ulster-Scots language.

AG Lyttle (great-grandson to WG)
Woking
2021

ROBIN'S RHYMES

1 "TO MY FRIENS"

Editor's note: In 1879 WG published his first anthology of short stories under the title of *Humorous Readings by Robin*. It was a new venture for him and he was anxious to connect with his potential readership, many of whom had only previously heard him on stage. So he included a Preface, writing to them in the broad Ulster-Scots of their "friend, Robin." These are the words he wrote.

TO MY FRIENS

My friens, it wuz at your requist
I got this wee book prented;
An' whun ye've read it till the en'
I hope ye'll be contented.
It tuk me mony a day an' hoor
Tae pit it a' thegither,
An' yit I hae as muckle left
As ocht tae fill anither.

So if ye'll jist dae what ye said—
Buy up them ivery yin—
I'll ken ye want tae see the nixt,
An' very suin begin.
I'm shair there's fowk wull lauch an' sneer,
An' say my book's a' "stuff"
That "Paddy" wuz a common boor,
That "Robin" is a "muff."

My friens, I didnae write fur fowk
That think themsels sae nice;
Wha's hearts—if they hae got sich things—
Ir jist like lumps o' ice.
My stories ir but little worth;
I ken that's very true,
But tak them as they come, my friens,
I wrote them a' for you.

An' mony an hoor they've help't tae pass,
An' aft it din me guid
Tae hear hoo hearty ye cud lauch
Whun I got up tae read.
Jist for the sake o' these auld times
I've put my book in prent,
An' if it pleeses you, my friens,
Then " ROBIN " is content.

3

2 "THE OLD TOWN CLOCK"

Editor's note: WG wrote this lighthearted poem, supposedly based on a conversation he had held with the town clock above the Market House in Conway Square, Newtownards. It was reprinted in *The Bangor Season* in 1885 so would have been in the *Gazette* sometime before then. Two years later—the clipping is c. March '87—he decided to start a Newtownards 'gossip' column with the Old Town Clock providing the gossip. The new weekly column always started with this verse:

"For a hundred years I've been looking down / By day and by night on this old town; / Speaking to men of the flight of time / As I ring out the hours with silvery chime; / And the square, like a huge stage, stands in sight, / Where no curtain falls save the curtain of night."

THE OLD TOWN CLOCK.
Newtownards

DEAR MR. EDITOR—You and I are old friends. It is a long time since we had that memorable chat which you kindly put in verse, and which I can repeat word for word. I saw you on Saturday last in the old Market Square, looking fresh and strong. You were talking to Mr. Greer Cleland and Mr. Martin Fisher. (You see I know everybody.) You looked up and nodded to me, for which I was very grateful, and began wondering whether I could not be of use to you in some way. For more than a hundred years I've been serving the townspeople. I may be removed some of these days, and I want to die in harness. So I have made up my mind to send you all the items of news that I can pick up, and I trust you'll print them. You know I can see and hear everything that passes, and many incidents come under my notice which are well worthy of putting in print. So here goes :—

I MISS the old North Downs very much. Dear me, how astonished I was the first time they mustered in the Square. Didn't I wonder what was up! They looked so solemn in their dark uniforms, and so awkward in handling their guns. Such guns! Why goodness knows what weight they were, and then what a jingling the men made with those iron ramrods. I'm told the North Downs will meet for training at the Warren, Donaghadee, this year. "Oor Tam" must look after them there.

THE OLD TOWN CLOCK

Of all the town clocks, tell me one can compare
With the clock that looks down upon old Newtown Square;
And where is the man who would wish to efface
The time-honoured lines of it 's honest old face?
Or alter the silvery chime of the bell
Of the old Town Clock that we love so well ?

Yet once methought that its race had run.
It had lived so long that its work was done;
That a grand new clock should be mounted there
To look down and smile on the old town square;
With great, round face, and with sonorous chimes,
In keeping with progress and modern times.

So I hied me away at a swinging pace,
From the High street down to the market place;
I climbed up the broad, old-fashioned stair,
And mounted the belfry loft with care,
Begged of friend Foster the door to unlock,
And show me the wheels of the old town clock.

Then he opened the time-worn door with care;
What wonderful pivots and wheels were there!
What great strong ropes, with connecting rod!
What ponderous sweeping of pendulum broad!
"The two-faced old thing!" I exclaimed with a frown,
"It is time we had got a new clock for the town."

The huge wheels paused in their dreary round,
With a curious, clicking, metallic sound;
And the pendulum broad, with its stroke so deep,
For an instant hung on its swinging sweep,
As up from the silent depths below,
A clear voice whispered—"Say not so!"

5

ROBIN'S RHYMES

Then Foster started with sudden fright,
And ask of me whether he'd heard aright;
But, e'er I could answer, the silence broke,
And once again the old clock spoke,
Its pendulum gliding again as of old,
And this was the story the town clock told:—

"For a hundred years I've been looking down
By day and by night on the dear old town;
Speaking to men of the flight of time,
As I ring out each hour with silvery chime,
With the old town square, like a stage, in sight,
Where no curtain falls save the curtain of night.

And many a strange life drama, I ween,
In that old town square in my time I've seen;
With acts that have frozen the oil on each wheel—
For a good town clock has a heart to feel—
Then do not remove me, for still I'm strong,
I love the old town I have watched so long.

Yet the town I first saw is not that of today;
Old buildings, like landmarks, are passing away;
But as old friends give place in men's hearts to the new,
So others are rapidly rising to view;
And I'm looking just now at the latest of all,
The bulwark of Newtown—the Protestant Hall.[2]

---

[2] These verses were written for an entertainment given in the aid of the building fund of the Protestant Hall.–Ed.

THE OLD TOWN CLOCK

But the people, the people, what changes are there?
As they eagerly gather to market and fair;
Or up the broad staircase so laughingly throng,
To bask in the pleasure of music and song,
Where are all the fair women, where all the brave men,
Who have reveled beneath me again and again?

Alas, they are gone on whose list'ning ears fell
The first merry stroke of my time-honoured bell;
I knew them each one, by sight and by name:
Watched them all, day by day, as they went, as they came
Till at length I would miss them, and face by face,
They all disappeared from the market place.

I have seen the babe, lying snugly and warm,
Pillowed to sleep on its nurse's arm;
I have watched it led out by its tiny hand,
And smiled at its efforts to toddle and stand,
While its sweet blue eyes lighted with wonder and glee,
As the chime of my bell drew their gaze upon me.

Swinging their satchels the children went by,
Up to my face turning every eye;
Oh, the old times! how they come back again,
No Intermediate or Model Schools then;
Old-fashioned people and old-fashioned rules,
Old-fashioned teachers and old-fashioned schools.

ROBIN'S RHYMES

Ringing out time with my silvery tongue,
Boys to men growing while yet I was young;
Girls who were children to women had grown,
Tripping along with sweet babes of their own;
Holding them high up to laugh upon me,
As they once had laughed in their innocent glee.

Old men and women with winter-white hair,
Pass and repass in the old town square,
And I note in their faces, which slowly turn up.
How deep they have drained from life's sorrowful cup
Some day they will come not, but passing instead
I shall look on the mourners who follow their dead.

* * *

But why should I talk in this maundering strain
Life is made up of glimpses of pleasures and pain
And none sees more gaiety surely than I
Perched up on the market-house ever so high
Two-faced!—never mind, there are men to be found,
Ay, and possibly women with faces all round.

Be that as it may, be it fiction or fact
Give me two faces more, and I'll never object;
I can see the old square, I can see to the train,
But a face east and west would be surely a gain.
Without turning my head I could then watch the Mayor
Who takes pains to enlighten the town and the Chair.

THE OLD TOWN CLOCK

I could watch how the editors handle the quill,
In harmony working and thinking no ill;
While out by Kiltonga and Bradshaw's old brae,
Where fond lovers ramble at gloaming of day,
I would see the dear creatures, oh, nothing I'd miss
Hear their vows of affection, their kiss upon kiss.

But I fear I am possibly asking too much.
Being two-face so long I'll continue as such;
But I pray you, good people, remember I'm old,
Winter weather is biting, and March winds are cold;
Within I am blest with kind Fostering care;
And Patton still keeps me in decent repair.

But I find it not easy, in seasons of late,
When a strong wind is blowing to keep my hands straight;
I could do it, I think, with a glass on my dial,
If you, my kind friends, would but give me a trial;
And when gas becomes cheap. I would ask you to place.
A nice little jet to throw light on my face.

Then by night and by day as you pass to and fro
The flight of the enemy, Time, you could know.
I've another request: tell friend Patton I pray
That a little more oil won't be out of the way;
Let him keep a supply of the best kind in stock
For age creeps apace on the old town clock

Just one word in passing: a friend may be old,
Yet his friendship more precious than silver or gold.
Never cast off a friend, though his face may be plain,
If his heart be alright and his life without stain.
Adieu, my good friend, I am weary of talk,
And I'm going to strike," said the old town clock.

3 "PADDY'S SANG"

Editor's note: WG went on to produce three volumes of *Humorous Readings*—stories that were mostly about two main characters, Paddy M'Quillan and Robin Gordon. He later decided to gather together all the Paddy M'Quillan stories into one new anthology which he called *Robin's Readings, Volume I – The Adventures of Paddy M'Quillan.* Robin was his narrator and in the story of "Paddy M'Quillan's Tae Perty" Paddy sings this song.

WG has Robin Gordon say, "A'll gie the words if ye can pit a tune till them, fur A beleev Paddy made it himself," thus confirming that WG was not quoting an existing song but that these were his own verses.

PADDY'S SANG

Oh, cum all ye boys an' girls so gay,
An' lissen well unto my lay,
An' if to wed you are inclined,
Some good advice in it ye'll find,
Ri-toor-a-loo-ral-ay.

Oh, when furst I met my Maggie fair,
My heart was fil'led with despair,
But I screwed my courage up one day,
And thus unto her I did say,
Ri-toor-a-loo-ral-ay.

"My lovely girl, with hazel eye,
For you I'd lay me down and a-die,
Oh, I'll buy you gold, I'll buy you pearl,
If you will fancy me, my girl,"
Ri-toor-a-loo-ral-ay.

Sez she, "Yer gold won't flatter me,
For to leev my ma an' go with ye,
For it's what I never intend at all
To go at any young man's call,"
Ri-toor-a-loo-ral-ay.

ROBIN'S RHYMES

Oh, I could not think for to go away,
So unto her I then did a-say,
"My hand is hard, but my heart is true
And I can a-fancy none but you."
Ri-toor-a-loo-ral-ay.

She said nae mair, but I saw her smile,
And she pulled at her apron strings awhile,
Then I pressed the damsel to my heart,
And said "My dear, we will never part,"
Ri-toor-a-loo-ral-ay.

So now my roving days are a-past,
An' the girl I luved is mine at last:
The bonnie girl that said me "nay"
Is my joy and blessing ivery day,
Ri-toor-a-loo-ral-ay.

4 "OH, MAGGIE DARLIN' "

Editor's note: In another story about Paddy M'Quillan, "His Courtship," Paddy falls in love and is inspired, for the first time, to write "poetry." WG moderates his skills accordingly.

Oh, Maggie, darlin', my love, my starlin',
My ain wee Maggie wi' the lauchin' een,
Yer the sweetest crayter, wi' the saft guid natur,
That auld Kilwuddy haes iver seen,
Och, my heart it's burnin'. An' me heid it's turnin',
A'm no worth leevin' nor fit tae dee;
A'll kill yer daddy, or my name's no Paddy,
If he'll no consent tae yer merryin' me.
A feel a' quer noo, an' my very hair noo
Wi' doonricht trouble is turnin' white;
My mind's tormented—och, a'm half demented,
An' a've lost my yince noble appetite.

5 "THE CHRIS'NIN' "

Editor's note: Because of—or perhaps we should say, in spite of—Paddy's attempts to woo Maggie in verse, the two were wed and in due course "wee Paddy" arrives to brighten their lives. At the close of a story called "The Chris'nin'," one of the guests at the christening party, Jeanie Brown, sings a song especially composed for the occasion. WG probably wrote it to a contemporary tune.

THE CHRIS'NIN'

Long Life tae brave Paddy M'Quillan, an' Maggie, his bonnie
     wee wife,
May they live here thegither contented and blythe a' the
     days o' their life;
An' may blissin's attend their wee Paddy we've helpit tae
     chrisen the day,
May he be a guid boy, an niver annoy, but his da an' his ma
     aye obey.

Shair Paddy's a kin' hearted fellow, ye min' hoo he made us
     a' laff,
Whun he tell't hoo he coorted Miss Norris that leeved doon
     in Ballymeglaff;
An' hoo he cud niver be gruppit, tho' Cuypid throwed mony a
     dart,
Till he met wi' his wee Maggie Patten, an' she ran awa wi'
     his heart.

An' noo that they're wedded thegither, may they niver know
     sorrow nor care.
May the sun iver shine on their dwellin', may they aye hae
     eneuch an' tae spare;
May we niver forget this gran' chris'nin', the tay, an' the
     toast, an' the feast,
An' may Paddy and Maggie invite us to a dizen mair
     chris'nin's at least.

6 " MAGGIE AND THE ROOMPAPER"

Editor's note: This is the first of three poems included here that WG wrote to promote businesses who advertised in his publications. It first appeared in 1885 in *The Bangor Season* as an advert for H. Thwaite Arnott, who was a Roompaper[3] Manufacturer in Belfast.

The following year WG included the poem in Vol III of *Readings by Robin*. The third line, "Whun a reached a weel-dressed wundey" reads, in the advert, "Whun a reached Thwaite Arnott's wundey."

Advertisements.

ROOMPAPERS.

A wuz in Belfast last Monday,
    An' oor Maggie made me stap
Whun a reached Thwaite Arnott's wundey,
    My! but that's the darlin shap !

Then nice goold and silver paper
    Very nearly made me blin' ;
An' a niver seen ocht chaper—
    So says Maggie—" Da, cum in."

In we went ; the mester knowed us,
    Tell't us baith tae tak' a chair ;
Brocht a pattern book, and showed us
    All the patterns he had there.

Sum wur plain an' some wur chackit ;
    Sum were floeered a' sae gran' ;
Hoo diz Mr. Arnott mak' it ?
    My, but he's the cliver man !

Maggie's yin there's nae refusin',
    But a lass can use her e'en ;
So a let her has the choosin'—
    'Twas a darlin' goold an' green.

My ! oor hoose, ye wudnae know it ;
    An' a tell the neibours a'—
Whun a bring them in tae show it—
    " If ye want yer hooses braw,

Jest gang whaur a bocht my paper ;
    Tell them what ye seen wi' me ;
Nae whaur can ye get it chaper "
    An' wi' that they a' agree.

H. THWAITE ARNOTT,
ROOMPAPER MANUFACTURER,
79 & 81 HIGH STREET, BELFAST.

---

[3] What we know today as wallpaper.

MAGGIE AND THE ROOMPAPER

A wuz in Belfast yin Monday,
An' oor Maggie made me stap
Whun a reached a weel-dressed wundey;
My! but that's the darlin' shap!

Thon nice goold and silver paper
Very nearly made me blin';
An' a niver seen ocht chaper—
So says Maggie—'Da, cum in.'

In we went; the mester knowed us,
Tell't us baith tae tak' a chair;
Brocht a pattern book, and showed us
A' the patterns he had there.

Sum wur plain an' sum wur chackit;
Sum wur floored a' sae gran';
Hoo diz the mester mak' it?
My, but he's the cliver man!

Maggie's yin there's nae refusin',
But a lass can use her e'en;
So a let her hae the choosin'—
'Twas a darlin' goold an' green.

My! oor hoose, ye wudnae know it;
An' a tell the neibours a'—
Whun a bring them in tae show it—
'If ye want yer hooses braw,

Jist gang whaur a bocht my paper;
Tell them what ye seen wi' me :
Nae whaur can ye get it chaper;'
An' wi' that they a' agree.

7 "DOMINIE HARVEY'S SONG"

Editor's note: In his novel, *Sons of the Sod*, one of WG's characters, a teacher, sings a witty song during a Punch Ball held near Carrowdore. He has written it all about the various locals attending the barn dance. Wesley, himself, in his youth, is believed to have entertained just such dance-goers in a similar fashion with some of his earliest comical poems.[4]

---

[4] See WG Lyttle's biography, *The Storyteller,* AG Lyttle, 2021

DOMINIE HARVEY'S SONG

Kind ladies and gentlemen, come listen to my song
It's of yourselves I mean to sing, so pray don't think it long,
For sure the world nowhere contains such people of renown
As the girls and boys that I could name, all in sweet County
     Down.

Now, first to give the preference, where preference is due,
There's a lady here to-night just sitting full in view,
Her name this night it is O'Neill, although it once was Brown,
And she's the fairest of her sex throughout old County
     Down.

And next there's bonnie Jeannie, who comes from off the
     hill,
Young Johnnie Hunter married her, and not against her will;
Oh, may God bless these two young wives, and never on
     them frown,
And may they every year increase the stock of County
     Down!

ROBIN'S RHYMES

Long live the Ballyboley boys, and flourish evermore;
And long live Wullie Yeaman, the Mayor of Carrowdore,
Who rubs his mare with wisps of notes when he's for
      Newton boun'
No richer man lives anywhere in all broad County Down.

There's the "Ballyboley Hoogher," M'Briar is his name,
And honest Sam M'Givern my notice too must claim;
There's Teugh M'Kay, and Morrow, too, who lives near
      Greyab town,
No man can better coffins make in all sweet County Down.

And then there's Hughey Hamilton—a boy so fond of
      cheese—
John Gibson who can stories tell that's always sure to
      please;
There's handsome Whulty Regan, too, that tailor of renown,
Who's fit to put his tapeline round the best in County Down.

DOMINIE HARVEY'S SONG

But if I spoke about them all, I'd keep you here too long,
There's just one girl I wish to name before I close my song,
The sweetest, dearest, brightest girl that ever wore a gown,
A marquis she could captivate, this maid of County Down.

Oh, dearly do I love this lass of Ballyboley Moss,
To guess the letters of her name you won't be at a loss;
If that dear girl won't marry me, myself I'll shoot or drown,
For she is all the world to me, this Queen of County Down.

Now, fill your glasses to the brim and drink with me a toast
"The ladies!' 'bless their loving hearts, they are our pride and
        boast:
Long live the O'Neills and Hunters, too, may joy their
        marriage crown,
Success attend the boys and girls of dear old County Down!

8 "RABIN'S AULD MEER"

Editor's note: This is the second of the "advert poems". It was published in Vol III of *Readings by Robin*, in 1886. It appeared in *Lyttle's North Down Directory and Almanac* as an advert for Mister Morrison's Wholesale & Retail Saddlery Establishment. "Saddler", in the 7th and 8th verses originally read, "Morrison." Written, as it was, prior to 1886, before the untimely death of WG's first wife, Lizzie, we can only wonder about her feelings that her husband's alter-ego, Robin, should have named his "auld meer" after her!

LYTTLE'S NORTH DOWN ALMANAC, 1886.

RABIN'S AULD MEER.

Ann Street Wholesale & Retail
SADDLERY ESTABLISHMENT,
BELFAST.

ROBIN'S AULD MEER

A hae got a grey meer, an' her name it is Lizzie,
Agen Krismas cums roon she'll hae seen thirty year;
The crayter, she's never content but whun busy,
An' there's no sich anither as Rabin's auld meer.

A bocht her in Santfiel' frae Tamas MacLeery,
Whun horses an' cattle wur no very deer;
A wush that my heart wuz as light an' as cheery
As the nicht a rid hame on the back o' my meer.

She wuz aye the gran' worker, baith Simmer and Wunter,
She kens ivery wurd that a say in her ear;
An' till this day she cocks up her lugs like a hunter
When she hears my fut cummin', diz Rabin's auld meer.

Yin day, a while back, a gied Peggy the hernish,
An' tell't her tae polish the buckles a' clear,
But she said that she neednae waste whitin' or vernish,
It wuz far ower shabby for Rabin's auld meer.

A kent by the luk o' her e'en what wuz cummin',
A wuz gie an' well used the same story tae heer;
So a lauched, and sez I, ' Very weel, Peggy woman,
A new set o' hernish a'll buy for the meer.'

ROBIN'S RHYMES

She's like yin o' oorsels, she haes been sae lang wi' us,
She haes wrocht for us mony a long day an' drear;
Nae man's goolden ginneys cud tak Lizzie frae us,
There's no sich anither·as Rabin's auld meer.

A went till Bilfast the very nixt Monday—
It's nae easy metter through thon toon tae steer—
An' jist as a reached Mister "Saddler's" wundey,
She stoppit hersel'—she's a wonnerfu' meer!

Mlister "Saddler" lauched an' cum oot till the fut-pad;
My errand till his hoose a suin let him heer ;
'The herniah,' he said , ' wuznae lukin' yin bit bad,
Still it wuznae the thing for auld Rabin's grey meer.'

A wush ye had seen the nice set that he showed me,
Sez I, 'Sur a doot they'll be far ower dear;'
He said he'd reduce them till me as he knowed me,
An' we wudnae fa' oot ower Rabin'a auld meer.

A can tell ye, my freen's, that a got rael guid velye;
Whun Lizzie gets dressed in her bonnie new gear,
She's as prood as a paycook, an' as shair as I tell ye,
She luks ten year yunger, dis Rabin's auld meer.

24

9 "PEGGY"

Editor's note: This love poem appears in *Humorous Readings by Robin Vol I*. It is very different from "Oh, Maggie Darlin', the youthful efforts of a lovelorn Paddy M'Quillan. In "Peggy," Robin Gordon is already of advancing years, as he talks endearingly to his Peggy, herself no longer young

ROBIN'S RHYMES

Had iver man a heart sae true,
Sae fond, as ye've bestowed on me?
Oh, Peggy, wur it no for you,
I'd lay me doon this day an' dee.

Its mony a day an' mony a year,
Since first I saw yer bonnie face;
There's nae yin else my heart can cheer,
There's nane cud fill my Peggy's place.

I min' it weel, I min' it weel,
An' niver, niver can forget,
The saft, sly luks I saw ye steal
At me the day when furst we met.

Yer black e'e beamed sae bricht an' cleer,
Yer hair wuz like the raven's wing;
Nae music iver charmed my ear,
Like sangs that Peggy used tae sing

My heart's noo weary, fu' o' care,
For life's a scene o' strife an' trouble
A true an' trusty frien's but rare,
An' wurldly pleezure's but a bubble.

PEGGY

But whun my Peggy's at my side
Nae erthly care my heid annoys,
For she's my trusty frien' an' tried,
That shares my sorrows an' my joys.

My Peggy, ye ir young nae mair,
Yer cheeks hae loast their rosy hue
The hand o' Time has bleeched yer hair,
An' made deep furrows on yer broo.

Life's changin' scenes, affliction's smart,
Hae dim'd the licht o' Peggy's e'e,
But Time can niver tuch the heart
That aye has been sae true tae me

The wurl may turn its back and froon,
An' Fate my dearest hopes may blast,
Yin smile frae Peggy brings me roon,
An' droons the sorrows o' the past.

I pooer my troubles in her ear,
An' as I speek they melt awa,
Her kindly words my heart can cheer,
An' its frozen channels thaw.

10 "ADDRESS TO LORD DUFFERIN"

Editor's note: From "A Crack Wi' Lord Dufferin" that appeared in *Readings by Robin, Vol III*. Robin, as Chairman of the Ballycuddy Tenantry, was elected to write an Address in verse to celebrate the return of their landlord, Lord Dufferin, to his Clandeboye seat.

ADDRESS TO LORD DUFFERIN

ADDRESS FROM THE BALLYCUDDY TENANTS TO THEIR NOBLE AND DEARLY BELOVED LANDLORD, THE EARL OF DUFFERIN,

"May it please your kind lordship, your tenantry here,
Who ever shall hold you in memory dear;
Have come to present you with this short address.
The words may be feeble, but nothing the less
Are the love and respect which your lordship's good name
From the farmers who call you their landlord does claim.

Great nobles are waiting to welcome you here,
And the land is rejoicing to-day far and near;
From your tenants at home to the Queen on her throne
The name of the noble Earl Dufferin is known;
And the fame of your lordship has spread o'er the world,
Wherever the flag of old England's unfurled.

But while to the rich and the noble you're dear,
None can love you so well as your tenantry here;
By the light of our fires, on dark Winter's night,
We have read of your doings with pride and delight;
Yet, one tinge of sorrow remained through it all—
You were absent—away from your beautiful hall.

29

ROBIN'S RHYMES

We plough and we harrow; we reap and we sow;
We are rough and untutored; 'tis little we know;
Our hands they are horny; our clothes they are plain;
By the sweat of our brows a scant living we gain;
But our hearts can be honest, and trusty, and true;
And they still have been loyal and faithful to you.

May your lordship live long—free from trouble and care,
Fresh honours to win, and fresh laurels to wear;
May your lady—so noble, so gentle, so kind—
A pathway of roses this life ever find;
May your sons prove as great as their father has been,
For a better, old Ireland never has seen.'

Signed on behalf of the Ballycuddy tenantry,

Rabin Gordon, Chairman.
Wully Fereuson, Secretary."

11 "LORD DUFFERIN'S RETURN"

Editor's note: "A Crack Wi' Lord Dufferin" also includes this poem written on the earlier occasion of his lordship's return from Canada after relinquishing the Governorship.

This sketch of Lord Dufferin is reproduced from *The Bangor Season*. After returning from Canada, "Robin's" landlord served for a time in Russia before reaching the pinnacle of his diplomatic career as Viceroy in India.

Earl Dufferin, Viceroy of India.

31

ROBIN'S RHYMES

Oh, your lordship has come back again,
Across the wide and raigin' main;
Shure my heart wuz breakin' still to think
That the great big ship you were in wud sink.'
      Now, why did ye go for to leave us?

Shure never an eye was dry that day,
When you sailed away for Canadey;
There was weepin' an' wailin' in every town,
And every parish in County Down.
      Now, why did you go for to leave us ?

But it's now you're back no more to roam,
And your Countess waits for you at home ;
Shure her heart will swell and leap for joy
When her lord arrives at Clandeboye!
      Now, ye never more must leave her.

Oh, its proud we are, both old and young,
And your praises are on every tongue;
You stayed too long, but isn't it true
That you showed what an Irishman can do?
      And you'll not go again for to leave us.

12"THE CURLERS"

Editor's note: *Robin's Readings, Vol II – The Adventures of Robin Gordon* has a story called "Robin on Ice" about Robin's introduction to ice-skating. In it, WG indulges in a favourite technique of using the names of real friends and acquaintances when he has "Mister Rabert Keghey" (Robert Caughey) sing the following song. It is all about the individuals who took part in the curling each winter, when the lake froze over at Kiltonga, on Bradshaw's Brae just outside Newtownards.

ROBIN'S RHYMES

Oh, would ye hear what roarin' cheer
There comes with frosty weather, O;
Then come away to Bradshaw's Brae,
And spend a day together, O!
Brave Sibbald Johnston leads the way,
'Twas he first taught us curlin', O,
And never is his heart so gay
As when the stanes gang whurlin', O!

And then comes Mayne, George Dickson, Kane,
Hugh Simms, and Charley Russell, O,
With full a score, all in a roar,
And eager for the tussle, O!
We muster on Kiltonga rinks,
With brooms so light and handy, O,
No royal curler ever thinks
Of playin' fop or dandy, O!

A shot we try at "chap an' lie,"
At "hogs" we luk sae dreary, O;
Then fling the stane wi' micht an' main,
And "chip the winner" cheery, O!
Then when the game is played and booked,
The word is given, "Luncheon, O!"
Of Irish stew, so nicely cooked,
We all fall to the munchin', O!

Come, fill each glass, and let it pass,
To wet our thirsty whistles, O!
And here's a hand from Ireland
To Scotland—land of thistles, O!
For Johnstons give a ringing cheer—
'Twas they that brought the curlin', O!
And may they join us many a year
To help us at the whurlin', O!

13 "MY BRITHER WULLY"

Editor's note: WG completed his trilogy of short stories with *Robin's Readings, Vol III—Life in Ballycuddy*. This includes the story, "My Brither Wully," about Robin's brother returning home from America. The tale finishes with this touching poem that Robin had sent to Wully while he was still absent. WG was echoing the heart-wrenching feelings of many of his contemporaries who had loved ones far away on distant shores.

ROBIN'S RHYMES

A wush ye wud cum hame, Wully,
A'm langin' ivery day;
There's naethin' been the same, Wully,
Since ye went away.
A sumtimes think if A cud mak
My wae across the sea,
A'd sling my bunnel on my back,
An' a' ahint me lee.

Fowk's hearts ir kureyus things, Wully,
An' a' can tell their tales;
Fur ivery yin that sings, Wully,
There's twunty weeps and wails.
But mine haes iver yerned tae yours
Since we wur lumps o' boys;
An' Wully's troubles aye wur *oors*,
An' sae wur Wully's joys.

A ken we shudnae pine, Wully,
A ken it's wrong tae murn;
The han' that is Divine, Wully,
Can joy tae sorrow turn.
But, man, my trouble's hard tae bear,
An' sair hae A been tried;
A'd pert wi' a' my erthly gear,
Tae hae ye at my side.

MY BRITHER WULLY

A'm affen at the burn, Wully,
Whun A've an hoor tae spare;
Whaur oor heids we used tae turn, Wully,
Wi' castles in the air.
Ahint the limpit rock I stan',
An' watch the risin' tide;
Man, if the sea was a' dry lan',
A'd suin be at yer side.

I'd walk it ivery fut, Wully,
Tae shake yer han' yince mair;
But A think A'll see ye yit, Wully,
Sae A'll try an' no' despair.
There's sumthin' whispers in my ear
That the cloud will no' aye hing;
That the sun wull sum day shine oot clear,
An' the wee bit birdies sing.

A wush ye wud cum hame, Wully,
A'm langin' ivery day;
Naethin's been the same, Wully,
Since ye went away.
A'm gettin' auld, an' far frae stoot,
My hair's as white as snaw;
Cum, while A'm fit tae move aboot,
Afore A gang awa.

14 "GOOD KING DAVID"

Editor's note: "The Ballycuddy Meinister" is another story told in *Robin's Readings Vol III*. Robin reads out to the other church elders a wicked piece of doggerel allegedly written by a disgruntled visitor to Ballycuddy Presbyterian Church while they were without a permanent minister. This is WG taking an irreverent and jocular sideswipe at church music and less-than-orthodox preaching.

> If good King David ever should
> Unto this church repair,
> And hear his Psalms thus warbled out,
> My God! how he would swear.
> Or, if St. Paul should chance drop down—
> From higher scenes abstracted—
> And hear his Gospels thus explained,
> My God! he'd go distracted!

15 "THE FARMER'S WIFE."

Editor's note: The following poem appears in *Humorous Readings by Robin, Vol III.* In it WG imagines a farmer's wife enjoying the just rewards of her toils.

ROBIN'S RHYMES

Oh, give me the life of a farmer's wife,
In the fields and the woods so bright,
'Mong the singing birds and the lowing herds,
And the clover blossoms white!
The note of the morning's heavenward lark
Is the music sweet to me;
And the dewy flowers in the early hours,
The gems I love to see!

Oh, give me the breeze from the waving trees,
The murmur of summer leaves;
And the swallow's song as he glides along,
Or twitters beneath the eaves;
The ploughman's shout, as he's turning out
His team, at rise of sun,
Or his merry good-night by the moonbeam's light,
When his daily work is done.

And give me the root and the luscious fruit
My own hands rear for food;
And the bread so light and the honey white,
And the milk so pure and good
For sweet the bliss of labour is
When the heart is strong and true,
And blessings will come to the hearth and the home
If our best we bravely do.

16 "THE BOBBY'S HAT"

Editor's note: The RIC (Royal Irish Constabulary) had just been issued with new hats—hard helmets topped with a spike. They were not universally welcomed! WG's fictitious police officer, Mickey Mulrooney, had plenty to say about it. "Mickey Mulrooney on the New Police Helmet" appeared in the third volume of *Readings by Robin*. It concluded with this poem.

ROBIN'S RHYMES

Oh, come all ye paple far and near,
From town and coun-ter-ee;
A doleful story you will hear
If you listen unto me.
Shure the wrongs of the force, they are well known ov
      course,
And their number none can tell;
But the last is the wurst, an' me heart's like to burst
For the ould hat I loved so well.

Chorus—For my ould hat it was nate, and it sat
So sedate-ly upon my head;
But och, a-lack-a-day! they have taken it away
And look what they've given me instead.

Shure my head wid pain it is loike to split,
For it's heavy as a hundred ov bricks;
And the wurst ov it is that the thing won't fit,
Let me try, how I may, it to fix ;
Arrah, what is it loike, wid it's grate big spoike
And a chain fit to hould a big dog;
Shure no wonder Phil M'Pake sez we've all made a mistake,
For the thing was clearly meant to carry prog.

Chorus—For my ould hat it was nate, and it sat
So sedate-ly upon my head;
But och, a-lack-a-day! they have taken it away,
And look what they've given me instead.

THE BOBBY'S HAT

Och, whin first I marched up the Shankhill road,
Now what do you think they said?
Why, that Isaac Nelson, they very well knowed,
Sint me that thing to wear on my head.
And they cried 'that's the hat for a big brick bat,
And the rows on the Twelfth ov July;'
While the younkers bawled out, 'Moike! what's the mainin'
        ov the spoike ?
Moind ye don't stick it into Biddy's eye !'

Chorus—For my ould hat it was nate, and it sat
So sedate-ly upon my head ;
But och, a-lack-a-day! they have taken it away,
And look what they've given me instead.

Och, the weather's hot, and I'm growin' fat,
And I don't know what to do;
If ye'll help me now to get back me ould hat,
Shure I'll do as much for you.
When I'm out on me bate, if your 'toight' on the strate,
Or looking after hours for a glass;
Shure I'll turn upon my heel, as slippery as an eel,
And I'll stale round a corner till ye pass!

Chorus—For my auld hat it was nate, and it sat
So sedate-ly upon my head;
But och, a-lack-a-day! they have taken it away,
And look what they've given me instead.

17 "SWEET HITHER DEW"

Editor's note: Heather Dew was a particularly fine Scotch Whisky distilled by the Mitchell Brothers who had premises in both Belfast and Glasgow. They advertised in WG's publications. This brief poem in praise of the fine liquor is from "Mickey Mulrooney on Heather Dew,"[5] one of WG's short stories quite likely originally sponsored by the Mitchells.

---

[5] See *Robin's Further Readings* by WG Lyttle, AG Lyttle, 2021

SWEET HITHER DEW

An' its och, if I knew
Where the brown heather grew
That is wet wid the dew
Biddy kapes in her bottle—

I wud spind all me days
Lyin' there at me aise,
An' whiniver I'd plaise
I wad moisten me throttle,

Shure no liquor they brew
Can excel Hither Dew!
Then hurray for the Dew, boys,
The sweet Hither Dew!

18 "FROM BETSY GRAY"

Editor's note: For his novel, Betsy Gray, WG chose to follow a pattern common at the time and introduce each chapter with an appropriate quotation. The sources of these were many and various but, where a suitable verse failed to come to mind, he simply wrote his own, putting them within quotation marks like the others, as though they were taken from a longer piece. Out of the 43 chapters of the book, he provided the following eight "quotes" himself. Each, is attributed to "Lyttle" except for the one for chapter 9, which is attributed to "Robin" and written in Ulster-Scots.

FROM BETSY GRAY

Chapter 1 – The Smiddy at the Six Road Ends

THE PATRIOT BAND
"Sworn helpers of the patriot band
Who fight for home and fatherland,
Behold the brawny blacksmith's strike
With heavy, swift, and ringing blows,
As fierce the smiddy fire glows,
And fashion out the deadly pike."

Chapter 6 – A Cruel Deed

REMEMBER ORR!
"Ay, ye may do your worst," he cried;
"My very heart strings you may sever,
Remember Orr! For us he died—
Shall I be an informer? Never!"

Chapter 9 – Mat M'Clenaghan's Conscience

MY HEART IS SAIR
"My heart is sair, ay, unco sair;
Oh, losh! My stamach's racked wi' pain;
Oh, gin a wuz but sober, lass,
A niver wad get fu' again."

ROBIN'S RHYMES

Chapter 13 – William Warwick

AND THERE ARE CREATURES
"And there are creatures, in the form of men,
Who crawl, as reptiles crawl, upon the earth,
They breathe but poison. 'Tis beyond our ken
If ought save Hell e'er smiled upon their birth."

Chapter 16 – Off the Track

COME WEAL, COME WOE
"Come weal, come woe, while this right hand
Can wield my broad sword, here I stand."

Chapter 17 – The Widow's Curse

A WICKED DEED
"A wicked deed, in truth, a wicked deed,
For this my country's heart shall one day bleed!"

Chapter 20 – Rev. William Steel Dickson

GENEROUS HEART AND NOBLE MIND
"A man of generous heart and noble mind!
A man whose like we ne're again may find."

Chapter 42 – The Execution of Warwick

OUT OF THE TYRANT'S POWER!
"Out of the tyrant's power! Free from the scourge of the rod!
Gone to a holier region; safe with the martyr's God."

19 "HOW TO WRITE TO THE EDITOR"

Editor's note: In this clipping from the *North Down Herald and Bangor Gazette* WG exhorts his correspondents to write clearly and we see an example of his sketches, too.

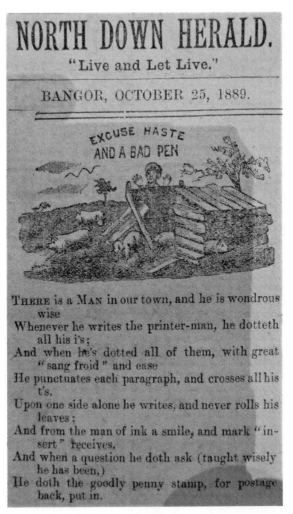

NORTH DOWN HERALD.

"Live and Let Live."

BANGOR, OCTOBER 25, 1889.

EXCUSE HASTE AND A BAD PEN

THERE is a MAN in our town, and he is wondrous
  wise
Whenever he writes the printer-man, he dotteth
  all his i's;
And when he's dotted all of them, with great
  " sang froid " and ease
He punctuates each paragraph, and crosses all his
  t's.
Upon one side alone he writes, and never rolls his
  leaves;
And from the man of ink a smile, and mark " in-
  sert " receives.
And when a question he doth ask (taught wisely
  he has been,)
He doth the goodly penny stamp, for postage
  back, put in.

HOW TO WRITE TO THE EDITOR

There is a man in our town and he is wondrous wise
Whenever he writes the printer-man, he dotteth all his I's;
And when he's dotted all of them, with great "sang froid" and
    ease
He punctuates each paragraph and crosses all his t's.
Upon one side alone he writes, and never rolls his leaves;
And from the man of ink a smile, and mark "insert" receives.
And when a question he doth ask (taught wisely he has
    been,)
He doth the goodly penny stamp, for postage back, put in.

20 "THE TANNAGHMORE HOLE"

A new piece by WG never previously published in any of his books

Editor's note: Like many County Down residents around 1884, WG was incensed at the apparent negligence of those involved in providing a new reservoir to supply water to Downpatrick. He wrote this 'lament' in the cumulative style of *The House that Jack Built* and printed it in his newspaper, copies of which, sadly, no longer exist.

Some four years later, and two years after WG's untimely demise, the legal ramifications of the fiasco were finally seeking resolution in the courts and the Tannaghmore Hole was back in the news. WG's widow, who had succeeded him as proprietor of the newspaper felt her late husband's skit was highly apposite and decided to re-print it. Fortunately, by then, copies of the weekly journal were being permanently preserved and so we have the text to publish in a book now for the first time.

THE TANNAGHMORE HOLE

This is the Tannaghmore Hole.

And this is M'Larnon, Contractor M'Larnon, who dug out the Tannaghmore Hole.

And this is Macassey, the clever Macassey, who instructed M'Larnon, Contractor M'Larnon to dig out the Tannaghmore Hole.

And this is the Bog, the wide-spreading Bog, the fathomless Bog, that was found by M'Larnon, Contractor M'Larnon, as he dug out the Tannaghmore Hole.

And these are the bones, the mouldering bones, of the horses and asses, the dogs and the cats, the puppies and kittens, that for centuries past have been flung in the Tannaghmore Hole.

And this is the water, the brown muddy water, that flows from the Tannaghmore Hole.

And these are the pipes, the Glasgow-made pipes, that convey to Downpatrick, the town of Saint Patrick, the brown muddy water, that flows from the Tannaghmore Hole.

And this is Sir Charles, knight valiant and bold, by whom it was told that the water was bad, the brown muddy water, that flows through the pipes, the Glasgow-made pipes, to the town of Saint Patrick, all the way from the Tannaghmore Hole.

And these are the people, the three thousand people, who must pay for the water, condemned by sir Charles, knight valiant and bold, by whom it was told that the water was bad, the brown muddy water that covered the bones of the horses and asses, the dogs and the cats, the puppies and kittens, that for centuries long have been flung in the Tannaghmore Hole.

And here are the Guardians, the Lords and the Commons, who meet once a week, in peace and goodwill, at the house on the hill, to provide for the people, the three thousand people who dwell in Downpatrick, the town of Saint Patrick, the women and men, the girls and the boys, and the infants in arms, who clamour for water, the brown muddy water from Tannaghmore Hole.

And here is their Clerk, so courteous and kind, so expert and sure, whose wonderful pen charms women and men with poem and song, and who grieves for the people, the three thousand people who clamour for water, but won't have the water, the brown muddy water from Tannaghmore Hole.

And here's Robert Hunter, the fearless Bob Hunter, the eloquent Hunter, who fears no man's face, and who laughs at "blue blood;" who fights for the people, the tax-laden people, and demands that M'Larnon, Contractor M'Larnon, shall dig out the Bog, the wide-spreading Bog, the fathomless Bog, and the mouldering bones of the horses and asses, the dogs and the cats, the puppies and kittens, that for centuries long have been flung in the Tannaghmore Hole.

And here is their lawyer—the Guardians' smart lawyer, so frigid and cold, with opinions worth gold, so learned in the law, large of brain, firm of jaw, and whose judgement declares that the people's affairs must be dealt with aright; that a bond is a bond when stamped, signed, and sealed; that the Bog long concealed must be brought to the light, no matter what plight the contractor be in. Just

54

think of the sin, the shame and disgrace, of giving the people, the three thousand people, who dwell in the town, Saint Patrick's old town, that brown muddy water that flows from the Tannaghmore Hole.

And these are the farmers, the hard bronzed farmers, the hard-fisted farmers, the Sons of the Sod; who sow for the rich man and sow for the poor; who toil late and early, in wind and in rain; who pay their rents gladly, and never complain of rack-renting landlords, but smile as they pay from the produce of praties and turnips and hay!

And here is the flax that some of them sow; ay, here is the flax that some of them grow, the green, waving flax from which linen is made, the flax that has built up Belfast's mighty trade; and they bury their flax in the Tannaghmore Hole, where it rots and decays.

And here is the Stench, the horrible Stench, so thick and so strong it would sole navvies' brogues, and it poisons the water, the brown muddy water, the oft condemned water of Tannaghmore Hole.

And here's Henry Smyth, the caretaker Smyth, who looks after the Hole, and the pipes and the pumps; watches every train to find Doctor Macassey, the clever Macassey, to prescribe for the people, the suffering people, the three thousand people, all dying from thirst, but who won't drink the water, the brown muddy water from Tannaghmore Hole.

And here is the Workhouse—the house on the hill—where the sick and the poor, the vile and the pure, the friendless and aged, the old and the young, the bad and the good, come for shelter and food, come to live or to die; the house where the Guardians, the Lords and the

Commons, every Saturday meet, in peace and goodwill, to provide for the people, the three thousand people who dwell in Downpatrick, the town of Saint Patrick, the women and men, the girls and the boys, and the infants in arms, who clamour for water, God's pure distilled water, but who won't drink the water, the brown muddy water of Tannaghmore Hole.

And here is the train, the fast-running train, which the Doctor should come by, and yet he don't come; for he's sick of his patient, he's sick, heart and soul, of the whole of the Guardians and Tannaghmore Hole. But he sends a prescription, a big long prescription—you'll see it just now—and adds a "P.S." to say, "This is my last, and now I withdraw from the Tannaghmore Hole."

And this is Fank Munn, the genial Frank Munn, whom Comber folk love, whose late elevation to Downpatrick Station pleased all of his friends; and who watches each train that comes from Belfast to see if the Doctor, smart Doctor Macassey, has ventured at last to come to the town, to set matters at rest, and to tell all the people, the three thousand people, that no one shall die by drinking the water, the brown muddy water of Tannaghmore Hole.

And here's the Prescription, the big, long Prescription, it weighs many pounds; it is corded and sealed, it is registered, too; shall we read it to you? *Not just now?* Very good.

And here is M'Allister, old Hugh M'Allister, bent with his years, stooped with age and with toil, who lives in the Union—the house on the hill—who loves to chew 'bacca, good strong plug tobacco, and who once blew the bellows, the ponderous bellows, to "bum" up the organ,[6] Cathedral organ, in worshipping God; now he toils up the hill, to the house on the hill, with the letters and parcels that come by the mail.

And here's old Hugh's bag, his old leather bag, for fetching the letters along to the House, the house on the hill; the old leather bag stained by time and the weather, gaping open at ends, burst right open at ends by that fateful prescription, that big long prescription, from Doctor Macassey, smart Doctor Macassey, for its bulk and its weight were so large and so great that it burst the old bag, the old leather bag, borne by hoary old Hugh, who never yet drank of the oft condemned water, the brown muddy water of Tannaghmore Hole.

And here's Robert Truesdale, poor old Robert Truesdale, who carted the sick to the workhouse long time, and who talked of the water, the Tannaghmore water, until his head turned; and he died of his grief, of his grief for the people, the three thousand people, a-dying for water, pure, heavenly water, and who won't drink the water, the brown muddy water of Tannaghmore Hole.

---

[6] To fill the organ's wind chest (using the bellows)

21 "THE BOSS OF BANGOR TOWN"

Editor's note: The occasion behind these lyrics was a banquet thrown by the Belfast builder, William Kerr, in August 1892. It followed the Grand Opening Ceremony of his new Victoria Road development in Bangor. The Town Clerk, Mr Pollock, was reported in the *Bangor Gazette* as delivering this song during the after-dinner speeches. The words attributed to the official, however, almost certainly flowed from the fertile and satirical mind of the paper's editor, WG Lyttle. References to the sewer fiasco, the board's attempt to close the fun-fair, their objection to a new pier and their chairman's involvement in the selection of a new minister for 2nd Bangor Presbyterian Church, all reflect items that had been lampooned in recent editions of the *Gazette*.

Oh, I'm the boss of Bangor, the boss of Bangor town;
I'm not Lord Mayor, I'm not a knight, but I'm a Proper Noun;
I hold the whip, I drive the team whichever way I please,
And I soothe rebellious spirits with a rub bullock's grease.
Then when I want to do a job that no one else will touch
Because it might be troublesome, or worry "such-and-such,"
The card I play still takes the trick—well nearly always so—
I write a wee "Memorial," and sign it, don't you know!

Chorus   It may not be in flowing phrase
             It may not be grammatical;
             Yet suit the people and my craze,
             Be terse or enigmatical.

THE BOSS OF BANGOR TOWN

It may be long, or even "square,"
Veracious and pictorial,
But, never mind, I'm always there,
To hand in my Memorial!

Should any builder want a sewer, and largely deal in bricks,
He should, of course, encouraged be, and never in a fix;
Should hobby-horses come to town and catch the people's
        pence,
Should certain people come to me to have them driven
        hence,
Should pleasure seekers from afar, who now and then come
        here,
Complain about our harbour small, and clamour for a pier;
Should rigid Presbyterians say—"We won't have so-and-so,"
I'll get a wee memorial and sign it, don't you know!

Chorus

Or if, again, some merchant-men who trade in our town
Should want the old Post Office brought somewhat lower
        down;
And nod and wink and say a lot of things I won't repeat,
A wee memorial I lay at Mr Shepherd's feet.
Just now the people cry aloud about congested sewers,
And blurt out, in their anger, "The fault, we know, is yours!"
So I'll open Main Street manhole, and just pop in below
Another wee "Memorial" both signed and sealed, you know!

Chorus

22 "BANGOR IN 1907"

"Read by the author (W. G. Lyttle) at a concert in Bangor
Good Templar Hall, 26th August, 1887"

Editor's note: In 1887, Wesley amused himself by imagining what may befall Bangor and some of it's more memorable characters twenty years hence. The significance of some of his references are lost now with the passage of time, but regarding others, readers familiar with WG Lyttle's biography, *The Storyteller*,[7] will still appreciate the sly digs he was making at his old friends—and adversaries.

Wesley used the poem on other occasions during that year, and in other towns, where he replaced some of the verses with others containing names and references familiar to audiences at each location.

The following year he included the original version in *Lyttle's North Down Directory and Almanac, 1888*, which is how it has been preserved for us to read now.

---

[7] *The Storyteller,* AG Lyttle, 2021, available on Amazon.

BANGOR IN 1907

I have a curious tale to tell tonight
You may pronounce it true, and may be right;
You may declare it bosh—be right again—
But hear it, first, and give your verdict then.

You've heard of Rip Van Winkle, he who slept
For twenty long, long years, and waking, wept
To find himself forgotten and unknown,
Dead to the world—forsaken and alone.

My story is more strange than his, I ween,
In dreamland twenty years I too have been,
The friends who knew me well in eighty-seven
Believe that I have long since gone to Heaven.

In the said year, on June the twentieth day,
I sauntered lazily round Bangor Bay,
Passed Sea Court's charming house and grounds, and then
My steps directed towards old Strickland's Glen.

The entrance to a cave I there espied;
Time-worn it was, wave-washed, and wondrous wide;
A sudden fancy struck me to explore
Where human foot had never trod before.

Crouched on all fours I passed the portal grim,
Crawled slowly on, the daylight growing dim,
The space enlarging then, I stood upright—
Stood but to fall with sudden, awful fright.

ROBIN'S RHYMES

A noise, like thunder, shook the rocky cell,
A flash, like lightning, struck me as I fell,
But here my lips are sealed, for what I saw
Is not for pen to write, or pencil draw.

This much—no more—I looked on boundless space,
Saw many a horrid form and demon face,
Heard these words still ringing in mine ears—
"Sleep, bold, bad man! Sleep thou for, twenty years!"

Here memory fades! How long in sleep I lay
I knew not then, and thought it scarce a day;
I woke, reclining by a bubbling stream,
And rising, strove to realize my dream.

The lovely lough lay shining, calm and blue.
The Antrim coast was full and clear in view,
But Bangor—could my eyes deceive me so!
Where was the town of but a day ago?

Great terraces, high turrets, streets miles long,
Big, towering steeples, bells that rang, Ding! Dong![8]
With mighty clang that rang o'er ocean far:
Huge, vessels in the bay like ships of war.

---

[8] Rumours were rife, at the time, of a new steeple that was to
be be added to St Comgall's C of I church in Hamilton Road,
which would eventually have a peel of bells.

BANGOR IN 1907

Bewildered, dazed, knees trembling, strength quite spent,
I sought the road, scarce knowing where I went,
I heard a step, and turning, saw advance
A man who eyed me with a searching glance.

"Poor man," he said, "you do seem weak and pale;
Where have you been? In workhouse or in jail?"
"I've been in neither place," I said in anger,
"I'm staying for the summer down in Bangor."

I told my story as I tell it now:
He raised one finger slowly to his brow,
And muttered, as he gravely shook his head,
"Poor man! from some asylum he has fled."

He led me to a cottage that stood near,
Gave me some bread and cheese, a mug of beer,
Then asked me where I lodged and who I knew,
"I live;" I said, " in Main Street, Number Two;

And I know all the people in the town,
Montgomery, Furey, Thomson, Neill, Smith, Brown,
Bingham, and Coates, and Ward, M'Cullum, Hall
But why go further—don't I know them all.

And then the boys at Pickie—Murray, Bell,
Sandy, big boy, who tells a story well;
Roden, "old party," with his pleasant look,
The Bolter, Buster, Booser, and the Duke;

ROBIN'S RHYMES

Dawson, the Masher, Jamison, M'Bride,
Who nigh broke Seggons' head against his side!
Good Billy Robinson, M'Kee and Yates
The slyest, but the jolliest of my mates.

Devlin, M'Cullin who recites so well,
(His sweetheart's name I could, if I would tell)
M'Connell, of the Bangor Swimming Club,
M'Kendry, of the cheery Mermaid pub.[9]

And Major Browne, so handsome, clever, gay—
'Twas he who planned the new bridge on the Tay—
Ah, 'tis a treat with him an hour to sit,
And hear his eloquence, his wondrous wit.

Dear Pickie, how I love the grand old rock!
So long resisting ocean's rush and shock!
Even Picton picked on Pickie for his dip.
And loves it as a sailor loves his ship

I know the fair Eliza—" "Stop!" he said,
"Most of the people whom you name are dead;
The figures, friend, which represent this year
Are 1-9-0-7, sure as we sit here."

---

[9] Wesley wrote a number of poems as advertisements for businesses who then paid to place the ads in his publications. *The Mermaid* was one such, about the "story" behind the name of Robert M'Kendry's "The Mermaid" Hotel in Bangor. *The Mermaid* also appears in the 1888 Almanac—as a poem, not as an advert. It is included in this anthology.

BANGOR IN 1907

"Then it is true" I said with falling tears,
"I've been asleep indeed for twenty years;
I had nor wife nor child my loss to mourn,
But someone, sure, will welcome my return.

Tell me, is good M'Kendry to the fore,
Who kept the pretty picture 'bove his door?
Who used to say we'd dress her head to tail
With rich red silk from Robb's big clearance sale.[10]

Is David Morrow living yet or dead?
Does Currell still preside at the Stag's Head?
Does David Erskin lead a single life,
Or has he taken unto him a wife?"

"M'Kendry's made a fortune," said my friend,
"And like good luck did Morrow, too, attend;
So they retired and live at quiet ease;
Erskin and Currell may do so when they please."

"Where's pious Scott?" "Oh, gone aloft, my man."
And Sammy Reavy, with his watering can?
Andy M'Blain, whose leg had a mishap,
(He roasted it) where's he? And where's Pee Yap?

---

[10] Robb's was a Belfast department store that carried Lyttle's anthologies in its book section.

ROBIN'S RHYMES

"All gone!" "And Archie Thompson, where is he?[11]
I used to read his pamphlets with such glee;
Eh, Archie was a lad! He made it hot
For Bowman and the other precious lot"

"Archie's an angel," said my friend, "with wings;
About him still we do hear curious things,
The people say from star to star he's roamin',
Alooking for M'Meekan and for Bowman.

The place has greatly changed in twenty years,
We now have seven splendid iron piers;[12]
Moore runs two dozen steamers, ay, does he,
To Bangor, Larne, Glenarm, and Donaghadee.

Piers are at Helen's Bay, Whitehead, Millisle,
There's one at Holywood this good long while,
John Moore is much admired everywhere,
He's now 'Sir John,' and of Belfast the Mayor.

We've penny trams that run to Crawfordsburn,
And Ballyholme—oh, everywhere you turn;
Trains to Belfast are sixpence, either way,
A horse and car cost but five bob a day."

---

[11] Archibald Thompson was a notorious figure in Bangor who got himself elected to the Board of Commissioners and made life difficult for James Bowman, the chairman—and enabled Lyttle to write many column inches in his newspaper reporting and poking fun at the perceived shortcomings of the Town Commissioners.

[12] The Town Commissioners had been dragging their heels over a decision to provide a longer pier to allow boats to dock in deeper water.

BANGOR IN 1907

"You had a paper here, 'twas called Gazette,
Have you it still? Is Lyttle living yet?"
"We have the paper still amongst us here,
I'm told 'tis worth five thousand pounds a year.

By Lyttle, some ten years ago, 'twas sold,
He went abroad, is living yet I'm told;
Some say he's dead and gone where such men go;
All Editors, I'm told, are sent below.[13]

At any rate one man in Bangor here,
(He wasn't fond of Lyttle it is clear)[14]
Said 'Lyttle's gone, and to a climate warm,
We needn't fear that he'll do further harm.'

He hadn't long said that till he died too,
And people said—I don't mind telling you—
He reached that place—if there is such an one—
Where coal is not imported by the ton!

Another thing you'll be surprised to hear,
The Town Clerk gets twelve hundred pounds a year;
James Rainey holds the post—a clever man,
What no one else can do, why, Rainey can.

---

[13] Lyttle was happy to include a joke at his own expense.

[14] A reference (as all his readers would readily recognise) to Lyttle's nemeses, the chairman of the Town Commissioners, James Bowman.

ROBIN'S RHYMES

Our population's ninety thousand; then
In summer you may multiply by ten;
Fifty hotels at least are in the town,
Three hundred spires three hundred churches crown.

We have a jail, I'm sorry that to tell,
And Sergeant Walsh—you doubtless knew him well—
Is Governor, and not considered dear
At what he's paid—six hundred pounds a year.

We've no disputes at any bathing place,
Sure twenty years ago 'twas a disgrace;
As in America, in summer weather
The lads and lasses all jump in together.

But poor old man, you're tired now of me,
You for yourself can all these wonders see;
Some other time we'll have a friendly chat,
And then I'll tell you more of this and that."

I asked what landlord now possessed the place,
He answered—while a smile lit up his face—
"Landlord! The word's from dictionaries struck,
That's why in Bangor we have had such luck."

* * *

BANGOR IN 1907

A thumping noise! A rude surprise!
The servant's voice, "Please master, rise!
It's, almost nine; I've called you thrice,
The 'Clandeboye' has whistled twice."

I woke to find 'twas all a dream;
To hear the steamer's last shrill scream.
So, having missed the morning boat,
Of this, my dream, I made a note,
And went to town at one fifteen—
I wonder what that dream can mean.

23 "THE 'MERMAID' "

Editor's note: This advert for M'Kendry's "Mermaid" Hotel in Bangor appeared in a number of Wesley's publications. The poem is also included, as a poem not an advert, in *Lyttle's North Down Directory and Almanac* for 1888. Although it is not absolutely clear, it would seem probable, that, like the other 'advert poems' this third one is also Wesley's work—unless we feel its promotion of hard liquor goes too much against Wesley's own teetotal stance. But he was a businessman and carried such advertisements in his publications, so why not profit further by offering his skill as a poet to the advertiser and write the text himself?

THE "MERMAID"

A Mermaid fair, with amber hair, and breast of spotless
    snow,
One summer's day, in Bangor Bay, swam swan-like, to and
    fro.
And all day long, she sang this song, till stars began to
    blink:
"O water, water everywhere! and not a drop to drink!

To hold the reins of sea domains, I am most highly favoured!
But the sweet sea with salt, for me, is rather highly
    flavoured!
I love a joke, like earthly folk: But in my briny palace,
A joke, like this is fraught, I wis, too much *cum grano salis!*"

So sang the maid, and loosed a braid of her luxuriant hair,
And round a rock she twined the lock, and lay at anchor
    there.
Then sank the sun, and one by one the stars began to peep,
And anchored there, by her golden hair, the mermaid was
    asleep!

But hush! an oar, from off the shore, sweeps softly through
    the bay!
And lo! a face of manly grace is turned the Mermaid's way.
A smile of light, a brow of might, behold M'Kendry stand!
A smile like Love, a brow like Jove, to threaten or command!

ROBIN'S RHYMES

On. on, he sweeps; the Mermaid sleeps; on, on, he gains
    the rock!
He stops, then lo! unfelt and slow, unbinds the anchoring
    lock;
His gentle arms entwine her charms, to shore he softly
    sweeps;
On, on they float; within the boat the unconscious Mermaid
    sleeps!

They reach the pier. A pearly tear slips from her slumbering
    eyes.
And now within M'Kendry's Inn the weeping Mermaid lies,
Between her lips, ambrosia slips—the immortal *eau de vie*;
And, as she takes, enchanted, wakes the Daughter of the
    Sea!

"Thou noble man! What language can convey my thanks to
    thee?
You saved my life; your loving wife how gladly would I be!
But since I cannot wed with man, in loving last farewell,
I weave my spell round all who dwell within this grand hotel.

Because you quelled my thirst, and held life's nectar cup to
    me,
May every draught which here is quaffed divine ambrosia
    be!
And since your "treat" was Brandy neat, as long as drinks
    endure,
May all within this noble Inn, be waterless and pure!

THE "MERMAID"

Of all you sell in this Hotel, from stout to *eau de vie*,
May every quart of every sort, a quart of guineas be!"
Then, with a look of love, she took a spangle from her tail,
"And may," said she, "your measure be upon a liberal scale!

All who have wealth, and value health, will wealthier,
      healthier be
If wine and beer they purchase here, and gin and *eau de
      vie*.
Your Whiskey is distilled bliss, and I pronounce your Rum
To be the best by man possessed, from Larne to Kingdom
      Come!

Farewell! Farewell! Preserve my spell, and prosperous may
      you be;
Farewell! Farewell! name thy Hotel 'The Mermaid,' after me!"
So sang the sprite; then passed from sight the Queen of
      Neptune's elves.
Spake she the truth? Old Age, and Youth! Step in and judge
      yourselves!

24 "BANGOR GOSSIP"

"Written for Entertainment given in the Bangor
Masonic Hall, November 16th, 1885."

Editor's note: It was a time when the long-ruling
Clique (as WG called them) of Bangor town
commissioners had finally been ousted and a new
board was seeking to manage their inherited debt while
still planning for future improvements. WG presented
this satirical poem to his fellow Freemasons about
what may (or may not!) be occurring. He pokes fun at
many matters that had all been reported in recent
editions of the *North Down Herald and Bangor
Gazette*.

He subsequently published the poem in his
newspaper and later included it in *Humorous Readings
by Robin, Vol III*.

BANGOR GOSSIP

They say we have gossiping everywhere,
That it lifts up from life a bit of its care,
That it purifies, rarifies, tempers the air—
With that you may not all agree:
But one thing is certain—we've gossips in Bangor,
The wagging of tongues counteracts winter langour,
I'll mention no names lest I rouse gossips' anger—
And don't say you heard it from me!

Some people could gossip and chatter for ever,
A mercy it would be their tongue-strings to sever,
They can tell by your eye—they 're so kitchenly clever—
What you've eaten for breakfast or dinner;
Should they single you out for their meddlesome chatter
They can tell who's your tailor, your grocer, your hatter,
And whether of late you 've grown leaner or fatter,
Whether you are a saint or a sinner!

The price of the carpet that covers your floor,
The errand of each one who knocks at your door,
All this they can tell to each other, and more,
They're so clever, so awfully clever;
But gossips can play at a dangerous game,
Flinging foul spots on a spotless fame,
Blasting for ever a once good name,
And friends, yea the dearest, they sever!

ROBIN'S RHYMES

Such gossips as these—if there are any such
In this North Brighton—I mean not to touch,
'Who knows what they'd say if I scolded them much?
Why there might be a horrible clangour!
'Tis all harmless gossip I've gathered for you,
The state of the town let us briefly review,
And what the new Rulers are going to do
For the town and the people of Bangor.

Some say that the fun at the Boardroom is o'er
That Commissioners in it will wrangle no more:
That the people with laughter won't wriggle and roar
While reading the *Bangor Gazette*;
But the gossips are shaking their heads and they say
That the newly-elected in office won't stay,
That the debts of the town they're unable to pay,
And the Clique may get hold of us yet!

Grave questions they ask that may interest you—
Who altered the Waterworks contract? And who
That sum of one thousand two hundred pounds drew,
The price of the waterworks puddle?
By whom was the building of markets delayed?
By whom are the debts of the town to be paid?
And what was the price of that nice silver spade?
Bless my heart, what a terrible muddle!

BANGOR GOSSIP

These matters of finance we need not review,
Some pleasanter theme I had better pursue,
And tell what some people are going to do—
But don 't say you heard it from me!
We're to have a new graveyard, a new chime of bells,
A splendid Town Hall an some nobby hotels,
A new Police Barracks, with plenty of cells,
Sergeant Walsh Sub-Inspector shall be!

Robert Legg will be made Rate-collector they say,
So our worthy Town Clerk gets a little more pay.
M'Cormick's wheel pump will be taken away
And presented to old Mr. Waddell ;
That big bill of costs for Election Petition,
If charged to the town would be foul imposition,
And could not be borne in its present condition—
Every horse is to wear its own saddle.

A magnificent spire the new church will crown, [15]
The Kinnegar wall [16]—that disgrace to the town—
Erected so strong that it won't tumble down;
The Carmen will have a storm shed;
We'll have plenty of water and plenty of light,
The pubs will be open by day and by night,
The police won't arrest you no matter how tight,
But carry you home to your bed.

---

[15] St Comgall's C of I on Hamilton Road
[16] A new sea-wall beyond Queen's Parade built along a previously unspoilt stretch of coastline

ROBIN'S RHYMES

They say that a new law will shortly be passed
To secure common rights for a much-abused class
Who dare not on Sundays indulge in a glass,
Or enter the door of a pub;
While rich men are swilling away at their beer,
Or sipping their whiskey and wine without fear
The distinction to me, I confess, isn't clear,
Twixt a publican's shop and a club.

From Grand Jury rule we intend to keep clear,
Our Rulers their own little vessel can steer,
Reducing taxation every year
Till it comes to a penny per pound.
They'll provide us with donkeys to trot on the sand,
Give music each night by a good local band,
Yet always have plenty of money on hand,
The hat they will never send round!

They'll do all you ask them to do, and far more,
They'll remove that old bathing-box—horrid eyesore—
From the front of our good Dr. Higginson 's door,
And cart it to Ballyholme sands;
Each door will be numbered, each street will be named;
Certain people with land-grabbing here have been blamed,
Who knows but the property yet may be claimed,
And the grabbers deprived of their lands?

BANGOR GOSSIP

The rotten old pier will be taken away,
And a new one put up during April or May,
And they say that at Clandeboye—now Helen's Bay—
A pier will be shortly erected;
That a large tract of ground has from Dufferin been bought,
That a township will quickly spring up on the spot,
With hotels, summer quarters, hot baths and what not—
The scheme has, no doubt, been projected.

When Moore's steamers start 'bout the middle of May,
With their colours all flying steam into the bay,
The town will be looking so fresh and so gay
That when Wilson's point they have rounded,
The sight of the pier will the heroes astound,
While the captain will shout as his quid he turns round—
"Boys there's no danger now of us running aground,
In fact it beats all! I'm confounded!"

Our handsome policeman—his name you all know,
Tho' the girls about Bangor admired him so,
In making a choice he was awfully slow,
But he's married and done for at last!
Now, wasn't it strange, with such lovesome girls here,
So charming, so handsome, so winsome, so dear,
That in courting, from Bangor his course he should steer,
And marry a girl in Belfast.

ROBIN'S RHYMES

Our Football Club here stands in high estimation,
And has caused among other clubs quite a sensation,
Who say the Bangorians lick all creation
With Captain M'Killip as Boss;
What kickers they are those who see them can tell,
As with spirit and grace they go at it, pell-mell,
Its capital sport though, and all very well
If you don't mind a kick or a toss.

To some other subjects I'd gladly allude,
But to bore you much longer just now would be rude,
On your gracious indulgence perhaps I'll intrude
On some other such night in this hall;
Now beware of the Gossips! they're dangerous folk,
And kindly don't say that the Editor spoke
One sentence about them save only in joke.
Good night, sir; good night to you all.

The End

This book is one of three companion volumes comprising:

Robin's Readings Volumes I, II and III omnibus edition by WG Lyttle (AG Lyttle, 2021) – WG's original "Robin's Readings"

Robin's Further Readings by *WG Lyttle* (AG Lyttle, 2021) containing twenty-seven more of WG's stories, including seven that have never previously been published in book form.

Robin's Rhymes, by WG Lyttle (AG Lyttle, 2021) an anthology of WG's poetry.

All three are available as print-on-demand, from Amazon.

They are released to coincide with the publication of the revealing biography of WG Lyttle—

The Storyteller by AG Lyttle (AG Lyttle, 2021)

81

The Storyteller

The improbable life of provocative newspaper editor, celebrated author and hugely popular stage comedian, Wesley Greenhill Lyttle.

The Storyteller by AG Lyttle (AG Lyttle, 2021) is available as print-on-demand from Amazon.

Viewbook.at/AGLStoryteller

Also by AG Lyttle:

Dillon's Rising
(AG Lyttle, 2016)

This historical thriller, set at the time of the Easter Rising in Dublin, is a tale of espionage, love and revenge, and one man's desperate struggle to survive six days of slaughter and carnage on the streets of Dublin that would change Ireland forever.
Available as print-on-demand ebook from Amazon

Viewbook.at/DillonsRising

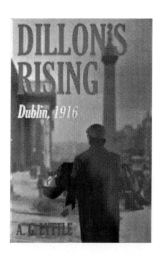

Glossary of Ulster-Scots Words

A

A (or a)	I (personal pronoun)
a	a (indefinite article)
a	have (as an auxilliatry verb)
a'	all
a'reddy	already
a'richt	all right
a'thegither	altogether
aback	to the back
aberazhin	abrasion
ableeged	obliged
aboon	above
aboot	about
abserve	observe
acause	because
acoont	account
adeptibility	adaptability
adjurned	adjourned
afeard	afraid
aff	off
affeckshinit	affectionate
affen	often
affrunt	affront
afore	before
Afrekey	Africa
agen	again
agenst	against
agglameration	agglomeration
agin	again
aheid	ahead
ahint	behind
Aiden	Eden
ain	own
airthly	earthly
aisy	easy
aither	either
aksept	accept
aksident	accident
akwant	acquaint
akwantenance	acquaintances
alane	alone
alang	along
Alick	Alec
alloin	allowing
alloo	allow
almanek	almanac
alow	below
altho'	although
amaist	almost
amang	among
amangst	amongst
Amerikey	America
ameytiffness	amativeness, amorousness
ammeters	amateurs
amoont	amount

an'	and	**auder**	older
ancitera	etcetera	**aukshin**	auction
ane's	one's	**auld**	old
angery	angry	**ava**	at all
anither	another	**awa'**	away
ann coar	encore	**awfu'**	awful
Annera	Andrews	**ax**	ask
Annerson	Anderson	**axed**	asked
anser	answer	**axes**	asks
anshent	ancient	**axin**	asking
Antick	Arctic	**ay**	yes
apeece	apiece	**aye**	always
apen	open	**ayont**	beyond
apoleygise	apologise	**B**	
appasite	opposite	**ba'**	ball
appertunity	opportunity	**backit**	backed
apren	apron	**bailie**	Scotish magistrate, bailiff
Ardgless	Ardglass		
argey	argue	**bailyee**	baillie
arithmetik	arithmetic	**baith**	both
arrah!	expression of excitement or deep emotion	**Baitty**	Beatty
		bakit	baked
		bane	bone
Arther	Arthur	**barefitted**	barefooted
ashair	assure	**bargen**	bargain
aside	beside	**bate**	beat or bet
athegither	altogether	**baynets**	bayonets
athoot	without	**be's**	is
athraw	awry	**beat tae**	must
attendit	attended	**beautifu'**	beautiful
attenshun	attention	**becase**	because
attribit	attribute	**becum**	become
atween	between		

beer	bear	**binch**	bench
beest	beast	**birl**	to twirl
beesum	besom, broom		around to go rapidly
beet	was (past tense of be)	**bit**	but
		biziness	business
beetle	round wooden mallet	**bizness**	business
		bizzin'	buzzing
begood	began	**black-avised**	dark-complexioned
behin'	behind	**blaw**	blow
behint	behind	**bleeze**	blaze
behold	see	**bletherin'**	chattering
bekause	because	**blethers**	nonsense
belang	belong	**bliss**	bless
beleev	believe	**bluid**	blood
Bellyclabber	Ballyclabber	**blunnerbush**	blunderbuss
Bellycuddy	Ballycuddy	**bocht**	bought
Bellyfooter	Ballyfooter	**bonnie**	pretty, fine
Bellygrainey	Ballygrainey	**booin'**	bowing
Bellygulder	Ballygulder	**boonty**	bounty
ben	in, into	**boords**	boards
berd	beard	**borrowfu'**	barrowful
berricks	barracks	**bothersum**	bothersome
betimes	occasionally	**bould**	bold
bewuldered	bewildered	**boun'**	bound
bewutched	bewitched	**Bowclick**	Beauclerc
bide	stay	**brae**	hill
bigg	build	**braid**	broad
biggin'	building	**braidth**	breadth
biggit	built	**braue**	broke
Bilfast	Belfast	**brauk**	broke, broken
bin	been	**brave**	fine
bin'	bind		

bravely	rightly, well	**ca'd**	called
breckin'	breaking	**ca'in**	calling
breed	bread	**Canady**	Canada
breeks	breeches, trousers	**cannae**	can't
breest	breast	**cannel**	candle
breid	bread	**canny**	carefully, fine, ordinary
breid	bread	**capten**	captain
brek	break	**carefu'**	careful
brekfast	breakfast	**carnapshus**	carnaptious
bress	brass	**catched**	caught
breth	breath	**cauld**	cold
bricht	bright	**ceevil**	civil
brig	bridge	**certun**	certain
britchin	breeching	**chackit**	checked
brither	brother	**chaiper**	cheaper
brocht	brought	**champ**	mashed potato with milk, spring onions and butter
broo	brow		
broon	Brown		
Broonlow	Brownlow		
brose	broth	**champit**	mashed
buddy	person	**chane**	chain
buddys	people	**chaney**	china
buffer	boxer	**chape**	cheap
bull-dug	bulldog	**cher**	chair
bulleyed	bullied	**cherge**	charge
bully	darling, sweetheart	**Cherles**	Charles
bumbee	bumblebee	**Cherman**	Chairman
bunnel	bundle	**chermed**	charmed
bye	by	**chew**	shoo! go away
by-ordinar	unusual	**chimley**	chimney
C		**chist**	chest
ca'	call	**chokit**	choked

choo / chou / chow	chew
chris'nin'	christening
chrisen	christen
Christyin	Christian
chucky	hen
chukit	chucked
claes	clothes
claith	cloth
clappit	clapped
clashes	tells tales; slaps
Cleekypatra	Cleopatra
cleen	clean
cleer	clear
clespet	clasped
cless	class
clip	mischievous or precocious young girl
cliver	clever
clod	throw
cloddit	threw
cloots	fragments of cloth
coast	cost
cocket	cocked
coffay	coffee
coffee-hoose	coffee house
coggit	wedged
comfurtable	comfortable
compenyins	companions
compered	compared
compleen	complain
compleent	complaint

compytate	compete
compytatin'	competing
condeeshin	condition
conduck	conduct
consate	pride
conserned	concerned
consert	concert
conshins	conscience
continye	continue
contranewity	contrariety
convaynient	convenient
conversityer-loaney	conversazione
coo	cow
coonsillors	councillors
coonsilmen	councilmen
coont	count
coonty	county
Coonty Doon	County Down
coorse	coarse, rough
coorse-voiced	coarse-voiced
coort	court
coorthoose	courthouse
coortin'	courting
corker	large pin
crack	chat
crack	chat
Craffurd	Crawford
crakt	mad
cram, crammer	a concocted story, a lie
crame	cream
crap	crop

craw	crow	**cushined**	cushioned
crayter,	creature	**cuver**	cover
crater,			
crather		**D**	
creddle	cradle	**da**	dad
creepy	low wooden	**dabbit**	dabbed
	stool	**dacency**	decency
cried	called	**dacent**	decent
cries	calls	**dae**	do
croobins	crabs	**daein, daen**	doing
croods	crowds	**daith**	death
crookit	crooked	**dale**	deal
croon	crown	**dannel**	dandle, nurse
croppy	nickname of		with an up
	an Irish rebel		and down
	in the 1798		motion
	Rebellion	**dannel**	move up and
cross-lukin'	cross looking		down
crowdy	meal of	**dannellin'**	dandling
	oatmeal and	**danner**	walk
	water	**darnae**	daren't
cruffles	a kind of	**daur**	dare, door
	potatoe	**daur**	door
cud	could	**daurnae**	daren't
cuddy	donkey	**daurs**	doors,
cudnae	couldn't		indoors
culler	colour	**daur-step**	doorstep
Culleradoo	Colorado	**day'l-agaun**	dusk
cum	come, came	**daylicht**	daylight
cumfurtable	comfortable	**daylusion**	delusion
cummand	command	**daysacrashin**	desecration
cummed	came	**daytermined**	determined
Cummer	Comber	**dayveloped**	developed
cuntry	country	**de'ed**	died
cupple	couple	**dealed**	dealt
curned	currant	**decaived**	deceived

ded	indeed	**dinnel**	throb, vibrate
dee	die	**dinneled**	throbbed, vibrated
dee	do	**dippit**	dipped
dee'd	died	**dipplemassy**	diplomacy
deed	indeed	**dipplematty**	diplomat
deef	deaf	**direckshuns**	directions
deefeekwult	difficult	**direkshins**	directions
deefened	deafened	**dis**	does
deein'	dying	**discoors**	discourse
deer	dear	**discuvered**	discovered
dees	dies	**diseese**	disease
deevened	deafened	**dislikit**	disliked
defeekwulty	difficulty	**disnae**	doesn't
deid	dead	**dispisishin**	disposition
deilment	devilment	**distraint**	restraint
dekerations	decorations	**diz**	does
deklare	declare	**dizen**	dozen
deleyin'	delaying	**dizn't, disnae**	doesn't
delicht	delight	**dizzen**	dozen
deliket	delicate	**Doag**	Doagh
denner	dinner	**doatin'**	doting, becoming senile
dependit	depended		
depertyur	departure	**dochter**	daughter, girl, woman
deppytashin	deputation		
derk	dark	**dokter**	doctor
dern	darn	**doktrins**	doctrines
desecrayshin	desecration	**dooble**	double
dezzled	dazzled	**dookit**	ducked
dickshunery	dictionary	**doon**	down
didnae	didn't	**doonricht**	downright
dinna, dinnae, dinnie	don't	**doot**	doubt
		dottered	tottered

GLOSSARY

drap	drop	**ective**	active
drappin	dropping	**eddykaishin**	education
drappit	dropped	**Eddyson**	Eddison
drawed	drew	**Edinburow**	Edinburgh
dreech	dull, long drawn out, dreary	**edykated**	educated
		een, e'en	eyes
dreedfu'	dreadful	**Eerish**	Irish
dreedful	dreadful	**efter, efther**	after
dreem	dream	**efternoon**	afternoon
Drimmon	Drummond	**efterwards**	afterwards
drippit	dripped	**eggziginseys**	exigencies
driv	drove	**egsakly, exakly**	exactly
droon	drown	**ekklesastyel**	ecclesiastical
dropit	dropped	**Elbert**	Albert
dug	dog	**eleck-trick**	electric
dumfoonered	dumbfounded	**elecktrickety**	electricity
dunch	dig, nudge	**elekshin**	election
dunin'	thumping	**em**	am
dunnered	pounded	**emn't**	am not
dunno	don't know	**en'**	end
dunt	knock, blow, nudge	**en's**	ends
duskit	dark	**encurage**	encourage
dyke	ditch	**eneuch, enouch**	enough
dyucks	ducks	**enimal**	animal
E		**enlichtened**	enlightened
e'e	eye	**envilopes**	envelopes
e'ebroo'	eyebrow	**epple**	apple
e'er	ever	**erches**	arches
echt	eight	**Erin**	Ireland
echteen	eighteen	**erly**	early
echtpence	eightpence	**erm**	arm
echty	eighty	**ermcher**	armcher

90

ermy	army
ern	earn
erth	earth
erth	earth
erticle	article
Erturs	Arthur
ertyfeeshal	artificial
escapit	escaped
eskort	escort
espayshilly	especially
esteblished	established
estymashin	estimation
et	ate, eaten
ether	either
exackly	exactly
excepshinal	exceptional
exemined	examined
exemple	example
expectit	expected
explainit,	explained
expleened	
expleen	explain
expreshin	expression
extrevagance	extravagance
F	
fa'	fall
fa'in	falling
failyer	failure
fair	far
faither,	father
feither	
fand	fond
farder	farther

fardins	farthings
fareweel	farewell
farl	flat cake of bread
fas	fast
fashin	fashion, way
fassen	fasten
faut	fault
favourit	favourite
fayver	fever
fear'd, feared, feer'd, feered	frightened, afraid
fechtin'	fighting
feer	fear
fella	fellow
femily	family
ferm	farm
fermer	farmer
fessin'	fasten
fether	feather
feyther	father
fiel'	field
figger	figure
fin'	find
finin', finnin'	finding
finnin	from Findon (Scottish fishing village)
fit	foot
fit-ba'	football
five-an'-twunty	twenty-five
flair	floor

91

flappit	flapped	**fould**	fold
flee	fly	**fower**	four
fleed, floo	flew	**fower-an'-twunty**	twenty-four
fleein'	flying	**fowk**	folk
flennin	flannel	**frae**	from
flet	flat	**freen, frien'**	relative, friend
flettin'	flatten		
flooer	flower	**freets**	omens
flooster	fuss	**frichtened**	frightened
floostered	flustered	**frunt**	front
floosterin'	fussing	**fu'**	full
fluir	floor	**fule**	fool
flurish	flourish	**fun'**	found
foarth	fourth	**funnygraff**	phonograph
foarty	forty	**fur**	for
focht	fought	**furbidden**	forbidden
fogets	forgets	**furbye**	besides
foondation	foundation	**furm**	form, platform
foondered	foundered, very cold	**furnenst**	opposite
forby, forbye	besides, also	**furniter**	furniture
forder	forward, progress	**furst**	first
forgie	forgive	**furstrate**	first rate
forgit	forget	**fursuk**	forsook
Forgyson	Ferguson	**fut**	foot
fornenst	facing, opposite	**futtygraff**	photograph
forrin	foreign	**G**	
forrit	forward	**ga**	go
fortnicht	fortnight	**gae (usu. gye)**	very, a lot
fother	fodder	**gae an'**	very
fottygraffed	photographed	**gaed**	went
fottygraffer	photographer	**gang**	go
		gangs	goes

92

GLOSSARY

gantin'	gasping	**Glesco**	Glasgow
gapit	gaped	**gless**	glass
gar	make, force	**glowered**	looked, stared
garr'd	made	**glowerin'**	looking, staring
gars	makes		
gassoon	young boy	**gluvs**	gloves
gaun	going	**goold**	gold
gear	goods, possessions	**goolden**	golden
		Gordin	Gordon
gebblin'	gabbling	**graip**	four-tined fork used in byres and stables
geeglin'	giggling		
geein'	giving		
gellery	gallery		
		graips	grapeshot
generashun	generation	**gran, gran'**	grand
gentilmen	gentlemen	**grandyer**	grandeur
gerd	guard	**grane**	grain
gerden	garden	**granwaen**	grandchild
gerdyins	guardians	**grape**	grope
gerners	gardeners	**grapin'**	groping
gether	gather	**grapit**	grabbed
gie	give	**grashis**	gracious
gie, gie an'	very, a lot	**grate**	great
(gye)		**greesugh**	glowing ashes, embers
gied	gave		
giein'	giving		
giely	greatly	**greet**	cry
gien	given, giving	**grewin'**	growing
gies	gives	**Greyaba, Greba**	Greyabbey
gingerbreid	gingerbread		
girnin'	moaning, making faces	**grisle**	gristle
		groun', grun'	ground
git	get	**grumelin'**	grumbling
glam	a sudden snatch	**grup**	grip
		gruppit	gripped,
gled	glad		

	grabbed
gude, guid	good
Guid	God
guidness	goodness
gulder	yell
gully	a large, coarse knife
gunpooder	gunpowder
Gunyin	Gunnion
guvernor	governor
gye (gie)	very, a lot
H	
ha'penny	halfpenny
ha's	halls
haddie	haddock
hadnae	hadn't
hae	have
haen	had
haenae	haven't
haes	has, have
haesnae	hasn't
hag	hack
haggit	hacked
hale	whole
half[-a]-croon	half[-a]-crown
hame	home
han'	hand
han'lin	handling
handfu'	handful
hankerchey	handkerchief
hannel	handle
hans	hands
happence	halfpence

happens	halfpennies
happer	hopper
happin'	hopping
happins	happens
happint	happened
happit	hopped
har'ly, harly	hardly
harmoneyum	harmonium
harrycuts	haricots
hasnae	hasn't
haud	hold
haudin'	holding
havers	foolish talk
Haybroo	Hebrew
hayroes	heroes
haythens	heathens
hearthstane	hearthstone
hebit	habit
heech, heegh	high
heecht	height
heed	head
heeds	heads
heer	hear
heerd	heard
heeve	heave
heffer	heifer
heid	head
heided	headed
heid-salts	head salts
heidstrang	headstrong
hel'	held
helpit	helped
helth	health

hemmer	hammer	**huft**	huffed
Henery	Henry	**huggit**	hugged
herm	harm	**hum**	him
herrin'	herring	**hungery**	hungry
herrins	herrings	**hunner,**	hundred
hersel'	herself	**hunderd**	
hervest	harvest	**hurrycan**	hurricane
heth	faith, indeed	**husselin'**	hustling
	(exclamation)	**I**	
hetterydox	heterodox	**ice bags**	icebergs
hev	have	**ignerance**	ignorance
hey	hay	**illeystrashins**	illustrations
himsel'	himself	**ill-wull**	ill-will
hin'	hind	**imaginashin**	imagination
hing	hang	**impayrael**	imperial
hingin'	hanging	**imperent**	impudent,
hinner	hinder		impertinent
hird	herd	**importens**	importance
hole-an'-	hole-and-	**impresshun**	impression
corner	corner	**indaykashins**	indications
	(secret)	**indaykorus**	indecorous
honner	honour	**individyal**	individual
hoo	how	**industris**	industrious
hooaniver, -	however	**Indyee**	India
inever		**infayrier**	inferior
hooer, hoor	hour	**informashun**	information
hoose	house	**ingin**	engine
hoots	fie	**Inglan**	England
hopit	hoped	**inklinashin**	inclination
horteykultur	horticultural	**insense**	instill, make
al			understand
hould	hold	**inspecter**	inspector
hoult	held	**insteed**	instead
houn'	hound	**instens**	instance
hudwink	hoodwink		

instrayment	instrument	**jug-jug**	jujube
instrukshin	instruction	**jumpit**	jumped
insubordina-	insubordina-	**jundied**	jossled
shin	tion	**junkshun**	junction
intae	into	**jurney**	journey
intenshun	intention	**K**	
interduce	introduce	**kail**	kale
intil	into	**kallyklashin**	calculation
invenshun	invention	**kame**	comb
investygaishin	investigation	**kamemyle**	chamomile
invitashin	invitation	**karat**	carat
ir	are	**Kaselray**	Castlereagh
Irelan'	Ireland	**katched**	caught
is't	is it	**keekit**	peeped
islan'	island	**kees**	quays
ither	other	**Keghey**	Caghey
itherwise	otherwise	**Keleyfurnye**	California
itsel'	itself	**Kelvinistik**	Calvinistic
iver	ever	**ken**	know
ivery	every	**ken'd,**	knew
iverybuddy	everybody	**kenned,**	
iverythin'	everything	**ken't, kent**	
iverywhaur	everywhere	**kenfer**	confer
Izek	Isaac	**kep**	block
J		**kep, kep'**	kept
jab	job	**kep'**	kept
Jaw Pee	JP (Justice of the Peace)	**kepin'**	keeping
jeneral	general	**kerd**	card
jest, jist	just	**kerekter**	character
jidges	judges	**kerpet**	carpet
jingel	jingle	**kerriage**	carriage
jirgin'	creaking	**kert**	cart
Joopiter	Jupiter	**kervin'**	carving

Keyhill	Cahill	**korderoy**	corduroy
kilt	killed	**kote**	quote
kin'	kind	**koughin'**	coughing
kin'er	kinder	**Kronikle**	Chronicle
kin'-hearted	kind-hearted	**kureyosity**	curiosity
kirkyaird	kirkyard, churchyard	**kureyus**	curious
		kye	cows
kist	chest	**kyte**	stomach
kitches	catches	**L**	
klashes	tales, gossip	**laberin'**	labouring
klum	glum	**laff, lauch**	laugh
knat	gnat	**laibers**	labours
knicht	knight	**laidle**	ladle
knichtit	knighted	**lain', laivin'**	leaving
knockit, knokit	knocked	**lan'**	land
Knocks	Knox	**lane**	loan
knowed	knew	**lang**	long
koffey	coffee	**langel**	fetter
koffey-hoose	coffee house	**lang-heided**	clever
koir	choir	**lang-tail'd**	long-tailed
kollekshin	collection	**lang-tongued**	loose-tongued
komishan	commission	**langwidge**	language
Komishiner	Commissioner	**larned**	learned
kommittee	committee	**lauch**	laugh
konduck	conduct	**lauchinstocks**	laughingstocks
kongreygashii	congregation		
konjuggelarity	conjugality	**lave, leev**	leave
konshins	conscience	**lawbreker**	lawbreaker
konsider	consider	**lazy-lukin'**	lazy-looking
konsiderashin	consideration	**learn**	teach
kontent	content	**leckter**	lecture
kontreydikshi	contradiction	**lee**	leave, lie
		leear	liar

leed	lead	**loas, loss**	lose
leek	leak	**loast**	lost
leeshins	licence	**lock**	quantity
leest	least	**lockit**	locked
leev	live	**lood**	loud
leevin'	living	**loonatic**	lunatic
lekter	lecture	**loused**	loosed
lempets	limpets	**lukit, luckit, lookit**	looked
len'	lend		
lerge	large	**ludge**	lodge
lern	teach, learn	**ludgin'-hoose**	lodging-house
Letin	Latin	**lug**	ear
letterly	latterly	**luggy**	wooden dish or bowl
lettytude	latitude		
licht	light	**luk**	look
lichtin'	lighting	**lukin'**	looking
lichtit	alighted, lit	**lum**	chimney, fireplace
lickers	liquors		
lickit	licked	**luv**	love
Lifftenant, livtenant	Lieutenant	**M**	
		M'Kome	M'Comb
liftit	lifted	**M'Queelan**	McQuillan
liker	likelier	**ma**	mum, my
likit, likeit	liked	**Mackerlane**	McErlean
limpit	limpet	**mainteened**	maintained
lint	flax	**mair**	more
linthole	pit for steeping flax	**maisles**	measles
		maist	most, almost
lippit	tasted	**Majisty**	Majesty
lissen	listen	**majurrity**	majority
list	enlist	**mak**	make
listin	listen	**male**	meal
loan	lend	**mangel weezel**	mangel-wurzel
loanen	lane		

manteened	maintained	merridge	marriage
Marlyborrow	Marlborough	married	married
maun	must	merry	marry
mauna	mustn't	mertherdum	martyrdom
mayjer	major	Mertin	Martin
meat, meet	meat, food	Mertin	Martin
meat hoose	eating establishment	mester	master, mister
mebbe	maybe	mesterman	masterman, boss
meedow	meadow	Methodeys	Methodists
meen	mean	metter	matter
meent	meant	Mewhunyee	Mawhinney
meer	mare	micht	might
Meer	Mayor	michtnae	mightn't
meeting- hoose	meeting- house, church	midden	manure heap
meetins	meetings	middlin'	middling, fair
Megimpsey	McGimpsey	mileeshayman	militiaman
megistrate	magistrate	mileeshy	militia
meinister, meenister	minister	milestane	milestone
meker	maker	militery	military
Mekonkey	McConkey	min'	mind, memory, remember
mem	ma'am		
memoryal	memorial	mindit	minded
mendit	mended	minit, minnit	minute
menner	manner	mirry	merry
menshin	mention	mishenary	missionary
Menyarry	Menary	mistak	mistake
Menyown	Menown	mither	mother
merbles, mervils	marbles	mizher	measure
merch	march	moartifies	mortifies
merkets	markets	moiley	hornless (cow)

99

GLOSSARY

mony	many	**needit**	needed
mooth	mouth	**needna,**	needn't
Moreyshon	Morrison	**neednae**	
morn's morn	tomorrow morning	**needulterates**	adulterates
		Neelson	Nelson
morrow	good day, next day	**neer**	near
		neer-be-gane	stingy, mean
mortyel	mortal	**neeves**	fists
MucKanally	McKinley	**Neevin**	Nevin
muckle	much	**neibor,**	neighbour
Mucklewane	McIlwaine	**neibour**	
Muckleyorum	McIlorum	**nervish**	nervous
Mucknattan	McNaughten	**nether**	neither
mullers	molars	**New-a-**	New Zealand
multiplicashun	multiplication	**Zeelan'**	
Munday	Monday	**new-**	newcomers
mune	moon	**cummers**	
muntains	mountains	**Newton,**	Newtownards
munth	month	**Newtownerds**	
murn	mourn	**Newtoonbreda**	Newtownbreda
musick,	music	**nice-lukin'**	nice-looking
musik		**nichered**	whinnied, snickered
mustashe	moustache	**nicht**	night
mysel'	myself	**ninnimy**	anemone
		nippit	nipped
N		**niver**	never
na	no	**nixt**	next
naebuddy	nobody	**no**	not
naethin',	nothing	**noddit**	nodded
naething,		**nomynated**	nominated
nathin'		**noncense**	nonsense
nane	none	**noo**	now
nater, natur	nature	**nor**	than
nayterally	naturally	**noshin,**	notion
needfu'	needful	**noshun**	

100

notis	notice	**onraysonable**	unreasonable
notised	noticed	**onrevillant**	irrelevant
nummer	number	**ontil**	onto
nurishment	nourishment	**ontruth**	untruth
nybers	neighbours	**ony**	any
O		**onybuddy**	anybody
o'	of	**onythin'**	anything
o'it, o't	of it	**onyway**	anyway
o'n	of an	**onywhaur**	anywhere
Oarem	Oram	**ooer**	hour
objeck,	object	**oor**	our
objekt		**oorsels**	ourselves
objeckshin,	objection	**oot**	out
objeckshun			
obleege	oblige	**ootdae**	outdo
och	expression of surprise, regret or resignation	**oot-gaun**	outgoing
		ootraijus	outrageous
och anee,	exclamation	**opeenyin,**	opinion
anee	of weariness or resignation	**opeenyun, openyin, opinyon**	
ochone (och-on-ee)	dear, dear!	**ordinar, ordnar**	ordinary, usual
		ordinashin	ordination
ocht	anything	**orfan**	orphan
odds	difference	**ould**	old
oer	over	**oursels**	ourselves
offendit	offended	**ov**	of
offens	offence	**ower**	over
offis	office	**owercum**	overcome
offiser	officer	**owerlukit**	overlooked
okepy	occupy	**P**	
on't	on it	**p'yin'**	paying
onless	unless	**pad**	path, road
onner	honour	**pamflet**	pamphlet

GLOSSARY

papper	pauper	**pickle**	small amount
pappit	popped	**picter**	picture
pardin'	pardon	**pied**	paid
parisence	presence	**pied**	paid
parleyment,	parliament	**piggin**	wooden
parlymint			vessel with
parritch	porridge		handle, for
parryfin	paraffin		milk
parryfrase	paraphrase	**pikter**	picture
parteekler	particular	**pileece,**	police
pashun	passion	**pleece**	
paydantik	pedantic	**pit**	put
peanny,	piano	**Pithygorus**	Pythagoras
peeany,		**pitin'**	putting
pianer		**pivet**	pivot
pea-pluffer	pea-shooter	**plantin**	copse,
peece	piece		spinney
peeler	policeman		(artificial)
peerie	spinning-top	**pleesant,**	pleasant
peeryodical	periodical	**pleesent,**	
peet coom	peat dust	**pleesint**	
peety	pity	**pleese**	please
peice	peace	**pleesent**	pleasant
peid	payed	**pleesent-**	pleasant-
pekyoolyer	peculiar	**lukin'**	looking
perambelater	perambulator	**pleeses**	pleases
peramelater	perambulator	**pleesure,**	pleasure
percel	parcel	**pleezhyer**	
perents	parents	**pleeze**	please
personallertys	personalities	**plekerds**	placards
pert	part	**plert**	heavy fall
pertikerlarly	particularly	**plester**	plaster
perty	party	**pletform**	platform
pickit	picked	**plew, ploo**	plough
		ploups	plops
		pluckit	plucked

pluggit	plugged	**prent o'**	pat of butter
plumper	vote (noun)	**butter**	
poasible	possible	**prepoas**	propose
poatry	poetry	**presarve**	preserve
pokit, pockit	pocket	**Presbytarian**	Presbyterian
polis	police	**primituve**	primitive
poo	pull	**pritta**	potato
pooer	power	**procla(y)ma(y**	proclamation
pooin'	pulling	**-shin, -shun**	
pookit	tugged	**prog**	food, grub
poon	pound	**promis**	promise
poorin'	pouring	**prood**	proud
pooshey	pussy	**protekt**	protect
posset	deposit	**Provedenshal**	Providential
poun'	pound	**Providens**	Providence
powl	pole	**provokashin**	provocation
powltis	poultice	**pu'**	pull
powny	pony	**pu'd**	pulled
pows	forelocks, hair	**pu'in'**	pulling
practis	practice	**public-hoose**	public-house
praisent	present	**puir**	poor
praisentashin,	presentation	**puir(-)hoose**	poorhouse
praisintaishin		**pun'**	pound
prangs	prongs	**purceedins**	proceedings
prappit	propped	**purcenter**	precentor
praties	potatoes	**purcession**	procession
praysentation	presentation	**purfessor**	professor
- shuntashin		**purlite**	polite
praysented	presented	**purshoots**	pursuits
precenter	precentor	**pursidin'**	presiding
preech	preach	**purtect**	protect
Preem	Prime	**purtend**	pretend
prent	print	**purtest**	protest
		purtiest	prettiest

GLOSSARY

purty	pretty
purvent	prevent
purvide	provide
puseeshin	possession
pye	pay

Q

qua(e)lifi-kashins	qualifications
quat	quit
quate	quiet
quatened	quietened
quattin'	quitting
Queenstoon	Queenstown, now Cobh, County Cork
queer, quer	fine, considerable, queer, strange
quer an'	really
querly	considerably
questyi(u)n	question
quoth	said

R

Rabert	Robert
Rabertson	Robertson
Rabin	Robin
rael	real
ragelarly	regularly
railins	railings
railly	really
raison, rayson	reason
rale	real
rapes	ropes

rashes	rashers
rassher	rasher (of bacon)
rattely	rattle
raw	row
raypresent	represent
raysedenturs	inhabitants
raysignashin	resignation
raytract	retract
reared, reered	reared, raised
rebbits	rabbits
red, redd	rid, free released
redd	read
reddy	ready
redeekilus	ridiculous
reech	reach
reedin'	reading
reeformayshir	reformation
reejeestered	registered
reejeestry	registry
reek	smoke
regerd	regard
reglar	regular
rekroot	recruit
relayshins	relations
releef	relief
releegin	religion
releeved	relieved
remarkit	remarked
remerk	remark
remoryals	memorials
rendezvoos	rendezvous

requist	request	**roon, roon', roun'**	round
resates	receipts	**Rooshin**	Russian
respectfu'	respectful	**roosty**	rusty
respek(t)	respect	**rote**	wrote
ressylushin	resolution	**rowl**	roll
ressytashin	recitation	**rubbit**	rubbed
restit	rested	**rubstrukshin-ists**	obstructionists
rether	rather	**ruck**	rick
returney	attorney	**rugh, ruch**	rough
revarse	reverse	**rumlin'**	rumbling
revitter, rivetter	riveter	**run**	ran
reyther	rather	**rung**	rang
richt	right	**S**	
richtit	righted	**sabbid, sabbit**	sobbed
richtly	rightly, well	**sab**	sob
rick-ma-tik	lot	**sae**	so, saw
rid	red	**saft**	soft
rideekilus	ridiculous	**sair**	sore, hard
rig	clothing	**saison**	season
rileroads	railroads	**samm**	psalm
riles	rails	**san'**	sand
rileway	railway	**sang**	a mild oath (Fr. 'blood')
rin	run, ran	**sang**	song
rines	reins	**sasser**	saucer
rivenged	revenged	**sate**	seat
riverence	reverence	**Sauny**	Sandy (Alexander)
riz	raised, rose	**saut**	salt
roar	cry	**saxpence**	sixpence
Rob(e)yson	Robinson	**saycondid**	seconded
rocht	wrought	**saycret**	secret
rockit	rocked	**sayperate**	separate
roomatics	rheumatism		

sayries	serious	Saturday	Saturday
sayri(o)us	serious	seyparate	separate
sayven	seven	sez	says
scaur	scare	shair, shure	sure
schule	school	shakit	shook
Scotlan'	Scotland	shamefu'	shameful
scould	scold	shampain	champagne
scrabbit	scrabbed, scratched	shan!	attention!
scraich	screech	shap	shop
screed	grate, grating sound	shapit	shaped
		shapman	shopman
scythestane	scythestone	sherp	sharp
seddle	saddle	sheugh,shougl	ditch, the Irish Sea
seedyrunts	sederunts (sitting of an ecclesiastical Assembly)	shew	show
		shods	metal heel-tips for boots
seegh	sigh	shooder	shoulder
seek	sick	shooer	shower
seekaterrier	secretary	shoon	shoes
seen	saw	shootable	suitable
seilin'	ceiling	shorthan'	shorthand
selery	salary	shud	should
selt	sold	shudnae	shouldn't
sen'	send	shug	shake
sergint, serjint	sergeant	shugar	sugar
		shuggin'	shaking
serkumstance	circumstances	shuggy-shoo	see-saw
sermin, sermun	sermon	shuk	shook
sertyfayket, sertyfecat	certificate	shunner	cinder
		shurt	shirt
servint	servant	shurtbreest	shirtbreast
servis	service	shuv	shove
seshin	session	siccan	such

sich	such	**sne(c)kit**	bolted. latched
sicht	sight	**soart**	sort
sign-boord	sign-board	**sobryety**	sobriety
sikafants	sycophants	**sodgers,**	soldiers
simmer	summer	**sogers, sojers**	
sinfu'	sinful	**sonsy**	stout and comfortable-looking, fine
sirkumstans	circumstance		
sirkus	circus		
sityeashin	situation	**soo**	sow
siz	size	**sook**	suck
skerser	scarcer	**soon, soond, soun'**	sound
skite	blow	**soople**	supple
skolerd	scholar	**sord**	sword
skringin'	creaking, grinding	**sorra**	not, nothing
skripters	scriptures	**sortit**	sorted
skuilhoose, skulehoose	schoolhouse	**sough**	long sigh or breath
skule	school	**sough**	rumour
skulemaister	schoolmaster	**souse**	the sound of a heavy fall
skyte	skate	**soverin**	sovereign
slaps	slops	**spauk**	spoke
slep'	slept	**spaycimen**	specimen, example
slicht	slight		
slippit	slipped	**spayshil**	special
sma'	small	**speek**	speak
smert	smart	**speer**	enquire, ask
smoothin'	smoothing, ironing	**spen'**	spend
smudjin'	laughing in a smothered way	**splendir**	splendour
		spree	adventure, frolic (often associated with drinking)
smuther	smother		
snappit	snapped		
snaw	snow	**spreed**	spread

squanerin'	squandering	**striv**	strive
squeeled	squealed	**stroup**	spout
stae	stay	**strucken, struk**	struck
staishin, stayshin	station	**stud**	stood
stampit	stamped	**studdy**	study
stan'	stand	**study**	steady
stane	stone	**stuk**	stuck
stap	stop	**stumak**	stomach
stappit	stopped	**subjec', subjeck, subjekt**	subject
startit	started		
steddy	steady	**substytute**	substitute
steem	steam	**suin, sune**	soon
steepin's, steepins	stipends	**suksessor**	successor
steers, sters	stairs	**sum**	some
Steevyson	Stevenson	**sumbody, sumbuddy**	somebody
steppit	stepped	**sumhoo**	somehow
sterve	starve	**sumthin'**	something
stied	stayed	**sumtimes**	sometimes
stik	stick	**sumwae**	someway
stimilatin'	stimulating	**sumwhaur**	somewhere
stiraboot	stirabout	**sung**	sang
stoopit	stooped	**sunner**	split
stoot	stout	**suppoas**	suppose
strae, stray	straw	**sur**	sir
strappit	strapped	**suree**	soirée
strate	street	**sut**	sat
strecht	straight	**suverins**	sovereigns
strechtforrit	straightforward	**Swade, swade**	Swede, swede
streck	strike	**swalla, swalley**	swallow
strenth	strength		
strickin'	striking	**sweemin'**	swimming
Stricklin	Strickland		

sweepit	swept	**teer**	tear
sweer	swear	**teerin'**	tearing
swep'	swept	**teeshy**	tissue
swutch	switch	**tek'**	take
T		**tell't**	told
tabaka	tobacco	**tell'tit**	told it
tableclaiths	tablecloths	**tenent**	tenant
tae	to, too	**terble**	terrible, terribly
taen, ta'en	taken, took	**terrin cottin**	terra cotta
taes	toes	**teugh**	tough
tak, tak'	take	**th', tha**	the
talkit	talked	**thankfu'**	thankful
talla	tallow	**thankit**	thanked
Tam	Tom	**theayter, thayeter, thayter**	theatre
Tammas	Thomas		
Tamson	Thompson		
tangs	tongs	**the**	they
tap	top	**the day**	today
tapcoat	topcoat	**the morrow**	tomorrow
tapitoorie	high pile, heap	**theer**	there
tappyyokey	tapioca	**theerfur**	therefore
taps	tops	**thegither**	together
targe	bad-mouthed woman	**theirsels**	themselves
tastit	tasted	**thems**	those are
tauk	talk	**themsel's**	themselves
tay	tea	**thenk**	think
taypot	teapot	**ther's**	there's
taytime	teatime	**thet**	that
teached	taught	**tho'**	though
teech	teach	**thocht**	thought
teegar	tiger	**thochtfu'**	thoughtful
teemin'	teaming	**thon**	that
		thonner	yonder

thoom	thumb	**tootle**	tooth
thoosan,	thousand	**trampit**	tramped
thoosan'		**translaters**	translators
thranyeen	straw	**traycle**	treacle
thrawin'	awkward,	**treet**	treat
	contrary	**tremenjus**	tremendous
thresh	thrash	**trevel, trevil**	travel
thriv	thrived	**trimlin'**	trembling
thro, thro',	through	**trimmel**	tremble
throo		**trubble,**	trouble
throogaun	active,	**truble**	
	energetic,	**trystit**	bargained
	lively, merry	**tuch**	touch
throoither	confused,	**tuk**	took, taken
	untidy	**tummel**	tumble
throwed	threw	**tuppence**	twopence
thumper	magnificent	**twa**	two
	specimen	**twa-an'-**	twenty-two
thunner	thunder	**twunty**	
thunnerstruck	thunderstruck	**twal-month**	year
thurd	third	**'tweel**	truly, indeed
ticht	tight	**'tween**	between
tift	tiff	**twuns**	twins
till	to, until	**twunty**	twenty
timmer	timber	**U**	
tinfu'	tinful,	**unce**	ounce
	mugful	**uncleen**	unclean
tippit	tapped	**unco**	very,
tither	other		exceedingly
tittivaitin'	titivating	**understan',**	understand
tollerated	tolerated	**unnerstan'**	
toon	town	**understud**	understood
toonlan',	townland	**uner, unner**	under
toonland		**uneyform**	uniform
Toonsend	Townsend	**unlerned**	unlearned
toother	state of		
	dishevelment		

unmennerly	unmannerly	**want**	went
		wantid,	wanted
unnateral	unnatural	**wantit**	
unnerstud	understood	**war**	were
uppermaist	uppermost	**wark**	work
urgan	organ	**warn't**	warrant, assure
usefu'	useful	**warst**	worst
V		**wasnae**	wasn't
valyeable	valuable	**wat**	wet
vegetaryan, -un, vegyterian	vegetarian	**wather**	weather
		watter	water
velue, velye	value	**wauken**	wake, waken, awake
ventur	venture		
vera, verra	very	**waur**	worse
vershin	version	**waurst**	worst
Victoryee	Victoria	**wecht**	weight
vinyerd	vineyard	**wee**	small
vittels	vittles	**weedow**	widow
vokil	vocal	**weel**	well
W		**weel-biggit**	well-built
w'ud, wad	would	**weelfare**	welfare
wa'	wall	**weel-informed**	well-informed
wae	way	**weemen, weemin, wemen**	women
waen	child		
waggit	waved, beckoned with	**weer**	wear
		weerin'	wearing
wake	weak	**weethin'**	somewhat, a little (lit. a wee thing)
walkit	walked		
walts	welts	**welcum, welkim**	welcome
wanner	wander		
wanrin, wanrin'	wandering	**well-tae-dae**	well-to-do
wanst	once	**welthy**	wealthy

111

GLOSSARY

wesh	wash	**whusker**	whisker
wesket,	waistcoat	**whuskey**	whiskey
weskit		**whuskit**	whisked
wether	weather	**whusle,**	whistle
wha, whae	who	**whussel,**	
whaiver	whoever	**whustle**	
wharaboots	whereabouts	**whusper**	whisper
whativer	whatever	**whustle**	a smart blow
whatsumiver	whatsoever		to the ear
whaur, whur	where	**whut**	what
whauraboots	whereabouts	**whuther**	whether
whauriver	wherever	**Whutley**	Whitley
wheatstray	wheat straw	**wi, wi', wid**	with
wheen	a quantity,	**wi'out**	without
	number	**wi't**	with it
wheesht.	hush	**wie**	weigh
wheest,		**win'**	wind
whisht		**winkers**	blinkers
whiles	at times,	**winna**	won't
	occasionally	**wint**	went
whin, whun	furze, gorse;	**wipeit, wipit,**	wiped
	when	**wipt**	
whuch	which	**wireyest**	wiriest
whulabaloo	hullabaloo	**Witherem**	Witherow
whumeled	turned over	**withoot**	without
whumle	knock or turn	**won**	win, won
	something	**wonner**	wonder
	over	**wonnerfu',**	wonderful
whunbush	whin bush,	**wonnerful**	
	gorse	**wonnerin',**	wondering
whungin'	whinging	**wonrin'**	
whuniver	whenever	**workhoose**	workhouse
whunny	hills covered	**workit**	worked
knowes	with gorse	**worl'**	world
whuns	gorse bushes	**wrang**	wrong
whup	whip		
whurl	whirl		

112

GLOSSARY

wraseld	wrestled		**wus**	was
wreckit	wrecked		**wush**	wish
writ	written, wrote		**wushers**	wishers
wud	would		**wusn't,wuzna**	wasn't
wuden	wooden		**wut**	wit
wudn't, wudnae	wouldn't		**wuthered**	withered
wuld	wild		**wuz**	was, were
wulks	whelks		**Y**	
wull	will		**yallaways**	or alloways, (bitter) aloes
wull-cat	wildcat		**yauk**	yoke
wull-fire	wildfire		**ye**	you
Wullie, Wully	Willie, Willy		**yeer**	year
wullin'	willing		**yer, yir**	you're, your
Wulyim	William		**yerd**	yard
wuman, wumman	woman		**yerdstick**	yardstick
wun; wun'	win; wind		**yerned**	yearned
wundey	window		**yersel, yersel'**	yourself
wunner	wonder		**yez**	you
wunnerfu', wunnerful	wonderful		**yin**	one
wunter	winter		**yince**	once
wur	were		**yirr**	growl
wurd	word		**yirrin**	yapping
wurk	work		**yirrs**	growls
wurkhoose	workhouse		**yis**	yes
wurkit	worked		**yisterday**	yesterday
Wurkman	Workman		**yit**	yet
wurl, wurl'	world		**yokit**	yoked
wurnae	weren't		**yon**	that, those
wurship	worship		**yoner, yonner**	yonder
wurth	worth		**yott**	yacht
wurthy	worthy		**younker**	young man, youngster
			yung	young

113

Printed in Great Britain
by Amazon